INSIDE

Understanding How Reactive Attachment Disorder Thinks and Feels

TIMOTHY L. SANFORD, MA

INSIDE: UNDERSTANDING HOW REACTIVE ATTACHMENT
DISORDER THINKS AND FEELS

Requests for information can be addressed to:

Info@LifEdvice.com

Editing by Aarin Harper and Callie Hovanec
Layout by Ed Hanks
Cover art by Dannie M. Wright
Cover design by Aarin Harper with LifEdvice.com
Interior diagrams by Timothy L. Sanford

2016 Edition (LifEdvice Edition) ISBN-13: 978-1534649477
2016 Edition (LifEdvice Edition) ISBN-10: 1534649476

TABLE OF CONTENTS

FOREWORD

As therapists, we don't always get to pick our specialties. Sometimes they pick us. Such was the case for me with Reactive Attachment Disorder. I have more than 25 years experience working with teens and adults and it's normal for any number of issues to be present, as varied as all the people sitting across from me. There were two recurring themes that I was unable to determine from where they were originating: (1) a deep inability, an incapability, to trust another person and, (2) the feeling of being in a literal state of survival constantly, even when the external circumstances seemed to be acceptable. These two themes were infused with intense reactions anytime, anything, even a small thing, seemed to rock the client's world. It was the reoccurrence of these intense reactions that ultimately landed them in one of my big blue recliners.

These two themes motivated me to gain an understanding of what I now realize is the disorder called Reactive Attachment Disorder. The primary purpose for my research was to better understand the thinking patterns behind the many outward behaviors I was seeing in my office. The content of this book is a result of that research. I have been working with those living with this disorder ever since.

What is It?

Simply put, Reactive Attachment Disorder (also known as RAD) is an infant's inability to attach to his or her primary caregiver – generally the mother – during the first 12 months of the infant's life. What adds to the confusion surrounding attachment are the words "bonding" and "attachment" get used interchangeably. In reality, they have very different meanings. The easiest way to describe the difference between these two concepts is this:

Bonding is what a normal, healthy (important adjectives here) adult will unconditionally (key word) do toward a child. <u>Bonding is adult toward child.</u>

Attachment is what a normal, healthy (important words again) child will conditionally (key issue here) do if and when the infant assesses its environment is safe enough and if the primary caregiver is consistent enough to be relied upon. The subjective measurement is the word "enough". The actual amount of "enough" will vary from one infant to the next even when both are in the same home environment and same or similar circumstances are encountered. <u>Attachment is child toward adult.</u>

To make things foggier, the primary caregiver may in fact bond, but the infant may still not attach.

Available Research

Most documentation on Reactive Attachment Disorder is geared toward parenting a child who has been diagnosed with this disorder. Many of these children have been adopted either from a foreign country or out of the foster care system; understandably there are often issues with attachment. What is being realized is that you can have a RAD child even inside an intact family unit. For any number of environmental reasons the process of attachment did not happen—infant toward adult. Additionally, the process of attachment may partially be there and hanging by a thread, only to be broken later by any number of circumstances such as the death of a parent, relocation or divorce.

The most widely noted circumstances causing attachment disorders are abandonment and neglect/abuse (any one or a combination of physical, sexual or emotional). Other situations that may increase the potential for RAD to develop in an infant are:

> Pre-mature birth with complications
> Traumatic pregnancy and/or delivery
> Birth mother's use of alcohol and/or drugs during
>> pregnancy
> After birth complications or trauma for the infant
> Lack of enough nurturing from mother
> Lack of enough validation from father
> Any number of early childhood traumas
> Any combination of the above

Don't jump to the conclusion that every adopted child or every pre-mature born infant has RAD. Obviously, that isn't the case. However, situations like the ones listed above would account for the times RAD exists when the child is a part of an intact family structure or was adopted at birth and taken home directly from the hospital to a good nurturing family.

Know too, that Reactive Attachment Disorder is a spectrum disorder. A person may fall anywhere on the following continuum:

MILD ←——————— MODERATE ———————→WILD

Not enough for an actual diagnosis, but the RAD thinking is still present and affecting the person's life and relationships	What we therapists call "full blown RAD" with the symptoms and behaviors that make the evening news

Diagnoses

I want to digress for a moment and explain what a diagnosis is and how professionals arrive at a diagnosis for any given individual. A diagnosis is a name for a particular, unique (in the true sense of the word) collection of symptoms and behaviors. Professionals use pre-established criteria to arrive at the diagnosis. The diagnostic name is then used to represent that collective set of symptoms and behaviors so we don't have to recite all the symptoms and behaviors each and every time we reference what is going on. A diagnostic title does not attempt to—nor is it intended to—identify where these symptoms and behaviors originated from or why they are present. Also, it is not intended to be a label with which to stigmatize a person.

Additionally, Reactive Attachment Disorder is a diagnosis formally reserved for infancy and childhood; which is correct. But, one doesn't simply "outgrow" the disorder with time. What happens is his/her behaviors change with age, which in turn, match a different set of collective behaviors and receives yet a different diagnosis – accurately so, mind you.

What I have noticed in my years working (psychiatric hospital, youth residential treatment center and private practice settings) is that underlying the other diagnosed disorders may be RAD. RAD may be (not always) the "starter domino" in the domino train of destructive thinking patterns and behaviors that finally bubble to the surface in a child, adolescent or adult. Dealing only with the end dominos (dysfunctional thinking patterns and behaviors) will have a lesser chance of generating deep, permanent change. Only when the "where" and "why" behind the behaviors are addressed can complete healing be possible.

As I present the issue of RAD, I'm not presenting it as the official diagnostic title for an infant's or child's set of unique symptoms or as a label placed upon the client. Rather, I'm using RAD as the catalyst, the source, the genesis, the starter domino that may actually be behind the symptoms and behaviors you are seeing and experiencing. I'm using the term RAD in a very broad over-arching manner.

This book is a compilation of the thoughts, reactions and belief patterns I have heard over the years from a number of clients who have RAD. It is representative of people across the entire spectrum from MILD to WILD, both male and female, teen and senior; whether officially diagnosed with a mental disorder or not. What follows, presented as Tom's Journal, is what all these said life is like for them as children, teens and adults.

Who / What Is to Blame?

Presently, our society seems intent on finding somebody else to blame for one's own foolish and immature actions. At the same time, there is a real effort to steer clear of the "blame the parents" defense. But who is at fault for all the chaos going on around you? Is it you? Your adoptive parents? Your biological parents? Who is to blame? Where do we put the burden of guilt? These are questions that deserve to be addressed from an objective perspective.

The balance point between "my parents are to blame" and "it doesn't help to blame anybody else for how I behave" will not be found if you approach it with an either/or mindset. The truth is—it's both, or several things collectively. Here's what I mean.

Made-up Scenario Number One:

> Gary's biological father abandoned the family when Gary was just 18 months old and his mother remarried quickly thereafter. His stepfather then physically abused him. His mother refused to believe him or do anything about the abuse when it was presented to her. Gary started using alcohol when he was 15 years old, which lead to fist fights at school and ultimately landed him in the state's juvenile detention system.

So who's to blame? And for what? Follow carefully as I try to explain.

Gary's biological father is guilty of abandoning his family and the impact that had on Gary.

Gary's biological mother is guilty of not dealing with her own childhood trauma, choosing to marry a man for her own insecurity's sake rather than what was best for the family unit, refusing to believe Gary and failing to protect him from his abuser and the impact that abuse had on Gary.

Gary's step-father is guilty of physical violence toward Gary and neglecting to be a positive parenting figure to Gary.

Gary is guilty of choosing alcohol as his coping tool (even though we can fully understand why he made that choice), the fighting and the impact of that choice got him expelled from high school and placed into the juvenile detention system.

Made-up Scenario Number Two:

> Emily was orphaned at the age of three when her Russian parents were killed in an auto accident. She had no extended family. She spent ten years in an orphanage where the staff did their best to care for the children even though there was insufficient funding to support the number of children they housed. Emily was adopted by a healthy, intact American family who has one other adopted child and understands the dynamics in adopted families.
>
> Emily is now an adult and recently got fired from her fourth job because she stole money. She had stolen money from all three businesses. The pattern of stealing began when she was in the fourth grade and she would take money from her parents—always denying it. Emily says it's her (adoptive) parents' fault because they didn't take her to therapy when all this started because finances were tight.

Again, who's to blame, and for what?

Nobody is guilty of the accident that took Emily's parents. The overpass that collapsed on them was one of many old structures in the city of Moscow. Life happens. Sometimes it's good and sometimes it's bad.

Nobody is guilty of Emily being orphaned and being placed in an orphanage. Life happens.

Nobody is guilty of giving her inadequate care. The orphanage staff did an acceptable job with the resources given them. Once again we see—life happens.

NOTE: If you're thinking "It's the government's fault for having such a terrible economy and not repairing the overpass or supplying more resources to the country's many orphanages!" Don't go there. It doesn't help Emily at all. It's part of the reality that things aren't fair much of the time.

To this point the only thing to "blame" is the unfortunate set of circumstances Emily was raised in.

Nobody is guilty of Emily being adopted into a nice family who understood her. Life happens, this time for the good.

Nobody is guilty of Emily's failure to receive therapeutic help. While it would have been helpful, her adoptive parents didn't do anything wrong by not being able to fund therapy for their daughter.

Emily is guilty of stealing, first food, then money, from her parents and her employers. Again, we can understand her actions when looking at her history and her need to look out for herself. She is responsible for the fallout from the choices she made.

The tendency is to be lazy and look for one piece of the puzzle to blame. It's not that easy, especially with RAD. Yes, we may give Gary and Emily more grace and leeway because it is obvious they did not get a fair shake in life. Unfair does not constitute guilt nor grant amnesty. This is a truth we don't like, or maybe want, to recognize. It reminds us of how little control we actually have. That terrifies many of us.

When you look at RAD, realize it is complex, confusing and intertwined with a number of symptoms and potential diagnosable mental health issues. Take care before assigning blame. Be careful before accepting blame too. If it's something you did, didn't do, thought, said, felt, or perceived, then the responsibility for that action/inaction does belong on your shoulders. Otherwise, it doesn't.

How to Read This Book

Rather than use different clients' stories to highlight different aspects of RAD, I have put all the thoughts, ideas and reactions into one story to keep as much continuity as possible. No one person exhibits all the thoughts, feelings, and behaviors that follow—not everything described here will fit every person. Keeping it all in a singular, first-person format will hopefully give you the best possible "inside" view of the mind of a person with attachment issues.

> I use a character (for continuity's sake) that I call Tom.
>
> He is a 49 year-old male.
>
> He was divorced ten years ago after thirteen years of marriage. He continues to have in-frequent contact with his ex-wife.
>
> Tom has one adult son who is an alcoholic and refuses to have contact with Tom.
>
> He was engaged three years ago to a woman six years younger than he. She broke it off after Tom became "violent" in her words.

Tom likes collecting and reading about guns, especially military types. He has a large number of firearms in his collection.

He works for a construction firm as a truck driver. He was demoted from supervisor to driver after years of displaying moderate anger issues toward management.

Tom mostly keeps to himself but explodes when he feels cornered or "attacked."

As for his family history:

Tom is an only child.

His father is a retired career naval aviator and was regularly deployed for six months at a time. When not at sea, he spent all his time aboard the ship working. He was, and still is, overbearing and has no patience with Tom.

His mother is a functioning alcoholic. She made sure she was strategically networked into the Navy wives social circle wherever they were stationed. She had no time for Tom.

She has a history of affairs, primarily with naval officers wherever they were stationed. Tom's mother kept the affairs quiet to appease her husband and Tom's father tolerated the affairs to protect his career.

One Naval officer she had an affair with (her husband's superior officer at the time) sexually molested Tom several times when Tom was four or five years old. When Tom told his Mother, she did not believe him. She slapped him across the face and told him he would ruin his father's career if he ever said anything to anyone about the incident, ever. Tom never told anyone.

When his father was stationed in Manila, Philippines, his mother would often forget to pick Tom up from soccer practice and he would walk home alone the three miles to base housing at night. On two separate occasions, boys from a local street gang beat him and took his soccer gear. Tom was between ten and twelve years old. This is when the anger and violence began.

As expected for a military family, they moved often. Tom stopped making friends at school. His family would be moving so why bother.

Circumstances and events like these happen to clients I've worked with. By using a compilation of many clients' stories in a one-person character, I keep the confidentiality that's mandated of me when sharing information I've heard in my counseling sessions.

The other character I created is Sandy, Tom's therapist. The specifics of her story are not important to the content of the book.

I change font size, style, use italics, underline, capitalization, blank spaces and pages in an attempt to have the reader experience the randomness and the "feeling" of RAD as much as I can literarily. This "experience" is just a sample of what the RAD person you know may be experiencing.

(Editors Note: The journal section has been described as exhausting, wearing, and "crazy making." **Please keep reading Tom's journal.** You will discover that Tom's journal moves from disorganized thinking to more organized thinking. I encourage you to remember that this is what it is like INSIDE

RAD; this is what it is like for someone with RAD, "*how RAD thinks and feels*". If you aren't the person struggling with RAD symptoms yourself, you are able to put down the book and take a break—some R&R [rest and recreation]. You can leave the jungle [the military metaphors will make sense later]. If you are the person with RAD or RAD-symptoms you may identify for the first time with another and have the experience of not being alone in the jungle.)

I share some of the current research on the subject of Reactive Attachment Disorder throughout Tom's journal for two reasons: (1) to present material on RAD to you and (2) to allow you to hear the response to that information from the RAD person's point of view.

My primary audience is the professional working as a psychologist, therapist, school teacher, youth worker, social worker, probation officer, etc. who encounters such a person in their line of work. My secondary audience is any friend or family member of such a person; to help them gain a better understanding of the dynamics of what's behind the behaviors they may see in a loved one. If a person with RAD reads this they/you may realize that they/you are not alone in what they/you are experiencing and that there is hope.

There is Hope

Several parents and clinicians who previewed this manuscript prior to its publication said the journal section, as mentioned earlier, was sobering, sometimes intimidating, exhausting, discouraging and often very intense. They wanted hope sprinkled throughout the book not just presented at the end. You will need to read through pain, anger, discouragement, confusion, and the "bad news" before getting to the hope. This is very intentional on my part in order for you to experience the strain and discouragement, wondering if there really is any hope. There is hope. It doesn't come as soon as you want—which is how the person with RAD has described it over and over again to me during the healing journey. There is hope. It will come—don't give up.

With that said, this is the world of the RAD person. This is a look *INSIDE RAD*.

INSIDE RAD

(Tom's Journal)

* Not sure how to start . . . except to start. Sandy told me to write down my thoughts and feelings during the week. She calls it journaling. That sounds girlish to me. I'll just write down my thoughts. Ok . . . Oh man . . . NOW My mind is spinning with all the things to write down – RIGHT NOW ! !! OK, let's keep steady. This won't be in any official order but these are the things spinning around inside.

* I guess I'll start with her suggestion to Google the DSM[1] (Diagnostic and Statically Manual). She said it's the "bible" for all psychiatric disorders. And look for a word . . . or diagnosis called, Reactive Attachment Disorder. Not sure why . . . but OK.

* Reactive Attachment Disorder is where a child doesn't attach to its mother. OK . . . so . . .

I don't remember enough of my childhood to know if this was there back then or not. I mean, I know Father was always out to sea doing his flying stuff as a Naval Aviator and Mother was always making sure she was at the center of the officers' wives social network. So even though I had food, clothes and "stuff" . . . Father was never around – and when he was "at home" he was never home . . . really. Mother was either at a social shindig or drunk or sleeping w/ some officer on base. I really don't remember much to know if this fits me or not . . .

Hummmmm . . . if I CAN'T remember much of my childhood AT ALL . . . and Father was absent as was Mother . . . Maybe the emotional needs really were NOT tended to . . . so . . . I guess this could have fit me as a kid. But nobody noticed it. I don't know.

* Met with Sandy today and asked her why she had me look up Reactive Attachment Disorder

(I see why they just use RAD!) She said it fits me and it explains all the crazy stuff I do that she can't seem to figure out why.

• OK, here's how Sandy explained things

NEED

TRUST

EXPRESS

MET
"Enough"

and here's the RAD pattern:

NEED

NO TRUST

EXPRESS

unMET

"Enough" for that particular child

When the child has a need . . . and then expresses that need in whatever way that child or infant can . . . and the need gets met . . . or at least met "enough" (that's the subjective term here) . . . then the child infers that the world is a safe place and that the primary caregiver is going to take care of them and they can then begin to develop a sense of TRUST in their caregiver and infer that the world is a SAFE place for them to be in.

> BUT . . . if the child has a need . . . and expresses that need, again in whatever way that child can . . . and the need goes Unmet . . . or at least UNmet often "enough" . . . it causes PAIN . . .
>
> Daha!

> and . . . no TRUST can develop because you never know for sure if what you need will be taken care of . . .

> Children . . . even infants . . . AREN'T STUPID !

So . . . what are the child's options? STOP
EXPRESSING THEIR NEED. Hello!
Children aren't stupid. You leave an
infant to cry in their crib long enough
and they <u>will</u> stop crying . . . hello! . . .
because . . . IT ISN'T BEING HEARD OR
ANSWERED . . .

Keep going . . . to have a need that goes
UNexpressed causes PAIN . . . again . . .

> So . . . what am I to do? STOP
> NEEDING ! ! !   Even though I
> really DO need I can't let myself
> need – because it's not SAFE to need
> . . . so
> I need . . .

> > but don't let myself need . . .
> > but I do need . . .
> > but it's not SAFE to need . . .

> > Sooooooo . . . I wall myself off
> >   from my needing as best as
> >   I can . . .

> > AND ALL THIS MAKES FOR AN
> > UNSAFE WORLD . . .

> > WHERE THE ONLY PERSON IN
> > THE ENTIRE WORLD I CAN

TRUST TO LOOK OUT FOR MY
NEEDS IS ME . . .

AND IT'S ME AGAINST THE WORLD . . .

NO WONDER IT FEELS LIKE A
SURVIVAL MODE . . .

BECAUSE IT IS . . . ALL THE
TIME . . . 24/7

365 DAYS A YEAR ! !

Makes sense to me . . . ! But I'm
confused about the attachment thing.
This seems to be talking about trust not
attaching to the parent.

* So the issue of TRUST is that it just
does NOT exist. TRUST can't even be
understood or imagined at all – not
really. When a person uses Erikson's first
Developmental Stage of "Trust verses No
Trust"[2] and ends up on the "No Trust"
side of the equation, it changes
EVERYTHING in the whole universe.
Sandy had me look up this stuff too.
She calls it "homework." It's OK, I don't
mind.

It's hard to put this into words because

it's a pre-cognitive, pre-verbal thing.

IT'S JUST NOT THERE, PERIOD . . .

It's not the same as knowing how to trust, but because you got "burned" a few too many times you're too gun-shy to extend trust again . . . it's the total inability to comprehend how to do trust at all. I don't think a person can fully understand the lack of _____?_____ (whatever the word is) unless they too have some sort of the RAD traits in them. Again, RAD is NOT "I know how to trust but I refuse to or am too scared to trust again."

NO!

I CANNOT . . .

     I DON'T EVEN COMPREHEND HOW TO . . .

    much less be ABLE TO DO it . . .

    I CAN'T.

      PERIOD!

* If I had to sum it all up, this would be in the primary MO for RAD =

     "The only person in this whole world I can trust to look out for me . . . is me . . . so I'll do whatever I have to do . . . right now . . . to take care of myself . . . thank you very much."

That's IT. THAT'S the driving _____?____ _____ (thinking / belief / force . . . not sure what to call it) . . . THAT'S the MO behind EVERYTHING they do . . . say . . . think . . . EVERYTHING . . . THAT'S IT . . .

     MO = Modus Operandi. That's Latin, I'm guessing, for primary "mode of operation."

* STUPID! I sound like an arrogant "expert" something, pretending to know all about a subject I just heard about 3 weeks ago. Idiot . . .

* And here's where therapy struggles and scratches it's collective head: How do you address and heal a pre-cognitive, pre-verbal wound with cognitive therapy techniques?

I know the answer to that . . .

YOU CAN'T . . .

> Daha. That's not rocket
> science . . .

* I can get the data to better understand
what RAD is all about, what it might look
like and even why it exists in me . . . but
how do I help heal the RAD? . . . Figure
out what's going on inside my own head?

UGGGH...

* She thinks RAD is a "hardwired" thing
in the brain and not a "fix-able" thing
. . . it can be compensated for or
adjusted to . . . but totally "removed"
from the brain . . . probably not – ever
. . . NOT what most people want to hear
she said . . . They want EVERYTHING
fixed nice and pretty . . . in a 30 minute
TV show length of time . . . Get over it . . .

* I can see the only SAFE is when it's all
OVER . . . and . . . it's not OVER yet . . .
so . . . I CANNOT be SAFE . . . EVER.

* ASSIGNMENT: I'm to write about, "What
the world looks like where there is no
– or very little (not "enough") – TRUST."

It is:

totally scary

and yet, not, at the same time

it's survive at all cost . . . and that's
where there's no time to be - or
rather feel - the terror inside

terror is "normal" 24/7 . . . 365 days
per year

but it's not SAFE to feel the terror
and since it's "normal" anyway
. . . you live with it like a small
pain from a little splinter in your
finger.

it's like war in the jungle . . .
at night . . .
in the rain . . .
in a firefight . . .
with the enemy . . .

and you don't
know who's
"friend" or who's
"foe" . . .

so EVERYBODY is a
"foe" . . .

or what's going to
happen next . . .

I'm just in the middle
of it all and I can't get
out . . .

because "life" goes from one night
time firefight . . . to the next . . . to
the next . . . to the next . . . to the
next.

And when it isn't a
firefight . . . you worry . . . and
listen . . . and listen . . .
and listen . . .

and wait because the
next firefight will jump on me if I
relax for even one moment.

I don't want to die.
"NOT DIE" is another MO.

I don't want to "live" if "live"
means "keep going" like this.

So I'm stuck in:
 "not die"
 "not want to go on"
 it's a real catch 22 . . .

which is a war in and of itself
being waged inside IN ADDITION
to the "war" on the outside!

* I think the body feels like it's in a
permanent state of shock . . . shock is
the body's way of coping with a trauma
in order to survive. When EMTs – or
whomever – come to rescue a person in
distress they treat for *shock*. The body
eventually comes out of the shock state
and begins dealing with the next line of
business, which is healing. That's the
normal pattern.

In RAD . . . YOU NEVER COME OUT OF THE
SHOCK STAGE . . . mentally or physically
. . . That's a little bit of what living with
RAD feels like . . . a feeling that RAD
equates to "normal" and "living" . . . and
"not dying" . . .

THAT'S ALL THE RAD BODY KNOWS . . . and
knows to know . . .

AGH!

BUT . . . and that's a really BIG "but" . . . that

> Jungle war
> > Survival
> > > Shock
> > > > "not die"

state . . . <u>becomes</u> "life" every day for RAD and that's "normal" for me. I was trying to keep this objective but it didn't stay that way. That's all I know. That's all RAD knows. And I never saw it that way as a child or even a teenager. I was clueless to all this stuff and thought life was fine. Maybe that was a good thing . . . maybe that was part of the NUMB . . . I don't know.

That's all RAD knows to know - and experience.

I've heard the talk about trust, safe, peace, friendships, family, etc., etc., etc. . . . but it's all just words - IT'S NOT REAL . . . and CAN'T be real in my thinking . . . ever . . . I know how to pretend and act that way . . . and talk that way . . . and even try to interact that way . . . BUT IT'S NOT REAL . . . And I have no knowledge of even how to make it real. I'm using capital letters sometimes because my mind . . . or my heart . . . is SCREAMING those particular words. That's the intensity I feel as my fingers try to keep up with my brain. NOTHING is sure . . . NOTHING is safe . . . NOTHING is guaranteed . . . NOTHING can be counted upon – until it's <u>over</u> . . .

then and <u>only</u> then will I know what's for sure . . .

* Sandy said last session that there is NO "object permanence" to speak of for me. And even if it's in my hand . . . "it ain't over 'till it's over" . . . because ANYTHING can go wrong at ANY moment . . . from ANY direction for ANY reason!!

THAT'S 1/1,000th of what it feels/thinks like (at best)

. . .

. . . <u>IS</u> like . . .

* Since NOTHING is secure . . . I can't trust/rely on/find comfort in the FUTURE . . . and . . . since NOTHING is secure . . . I can't trust/rely on/find comfort in the PRESENT either. There IS NO "comfort." There's just survival . . .

"don't die . . ."

* I can't find – or at least it feels like I can't find – the words to accurately de-scribe this . . . I want to keep writing but I don't . . .

Grrrrrrr. Sandy may be right; this RAD stuff sounds a whole lot like my life. That stinks!

* Mind memory = the data
   Heart memory = the emotions / feelings
   Body memory = the physical sensations
. . . somebody called this the "ab-reactions" the body feels.

It's "divide and conquer" so all 3 types of remembering of the same event are sent to separate/disconnected places from each other because it's TOO MUCH to be kept all together . . . It will overload the "system" . . . and since you "can't die"

. . . no matter what . . .

"Divide and conquer" becomes SOP
(Standard Operating Procedures) . . .

* It makes sense, like Sandy said, that
RAD is "hardwired" and not "fix-able" . . .
If certain brain links aren't developed at
the appropriate times in a child's
development they will likely never be
made. I mean, if you're trying to drive
to some town and the road you're taking
crosses over a bridge spanning a river,
and the bridge never got built . . . you
won't get there. You have to find an
alternate route across the same river
where there's a bridge. That's the "can't be
fixed" but can be "compensated" for part.

* Maslow's Hierarchy of Need[3] stuff fits
in here somewhere. If you don't have
the lowest levels met you can't go up
the pyramid. That sucks . . . because
with RAD I'm stuck on the lower 2 levels
all the time. I have my physical safety
needs met – if I look at it objectively
(but don't trust it) . . . but the "Emotional
Security" stuff . . . that's what RAD's all
about and it just isn't there . . . so who
cares about what the upper levels are and
what they have to offer . . .

* RAD people probably have <u>food issues.</u>

Maybe not an official eating disorder – because survival is our MO – but eating/ food issues . . . likely.

Eat too much, hoard food, binge (unofficially) when food (especially free food – like at a party) is available, or purposefully restricting . . . (some) food so you don't get too "dependent" on food,
etc., etc., etc.

Because NOTHING in the future is SECURE . . . and you need food to survive, you stock pile – either by hoarding or eating (so it's "stockpiled" inside you where <u>no one</u> can take it away).

"Grab the food you can when it's there because you never know when there won't be any more", is the voice in my head.

And is it any surprise how I can use food for "comfort" – like other people use food for comfort – like my donuts in my lunch bag during high school. That's why I got so outraged/out of control when they were stolen from my locker those few times. I can still remember it vividly today. Not only was my SURVIVAL FOOD taken away . . . so was my CONTROL . . . someone ELSE had the control . . .

which means I'M GOING TO GET HURT!

I don't know if RAD people tend to be picky eaters or not. Don't know about that.

* If there is a disconnect between the brain and body . . . the body may be UNDER FED because the brain doesn't hear – or refuses to hear – the hungry signals from the body.

And then there's the issue of RAD having a real issue with not being able to breathe. I always thought it was because there was a traumatic event of being choked or smothering or drowning. That may be true . . . but I'm wondering if it's exacerbated because AIR is a LIFE SUPPORT . . . back to

                    SURVIVAL =
                        FOOD
                        AIR

Maybe the breathing thing is a PTSD + RAD double whammy thing. The PTSD fits but it would fit into the RAD's need to survive too. Maybe that's why I'm very protective about anything near or around my mouth or nose. I can't STAND not being able to breathe and when I have a stuffy nose it's even worse because all I can think about is "half my airway is shut off and what if something happens to my ability to breathe out of my mouth?"

I just remembered. Mother told me – in a fit of rage one time – that I would go totally crazy as a child whenever I had a stuffy head at night and couldn't breathe through my nose. I was "inconsolable" and "irrational" she said – not that she ever tried very hard to console me anyway . . .

* To SURVIVE . . . you need:
                FOOD
                AIR
                MOVE
                ALERTNESS (always . . .

33

ALWAYS being on guard . . . on watch
. . . alert . . . watching . . . listening,
seeing, feeling . . . ALWAYS . . .)

NO WONDER RAD also results in sleep
disturbances many times. Daha!!! You
CAN'T let yourself fully sleep because
you have to stay on guard - even while
sleeping!

NO ONE HAS MY BACK . . . except ME!

So . . . poor sleep patterns
          all the effects of sleep problems
          @ times sleep SOOOOO deeply as
to "hibernate" (again an alternate
SURVIVAL technique, when I can't stay
alert any longer . . . I just don't exist .
. . that way I can't get hurt since I don't
exist . . .).

* Could that be why it's so hard for
people to startle me - because I'm always
waiting for it anyway?! . . . Hummmm . . .
Don't know. It makes sense that it would
be hard to "surprise" a person who's
ALWAYS on guard.

* To SURVIVE . . . you need:
          FOOD
          AIR

        MOVE
        ALERTNESS
        NUMB (Not feel so you can
keep going . . . no matter what the heart
or body feels)

* A DISCONNECT – a "divide and not die"
type of response

* In the same exact way PAIN is NOT the
enemy . . .
                        and IS the enemy

    – Not; because "I'll get through it"
    – Because; "It's gonna kill me!"

* If Ericson's Developmental theory[4]
idea of "being stuck" in the last stage
you didn't successfully navigate is true
. . . then SOOOOO much of what a person
needs to "learn" for "normal" living has
been de-railed with RAD . . . In a sense
they ARE developmentally delayed even
if never diagnosed with it.

Especially socially because who – in their
right mind – socializes in the middle of
a war in the jungle . . . @ night . . . in a
firefight . . . in the rain???

NOT ME . . .

Daha?!

* AND SINCE I don't always have control over:
> FOOD
> AIR
> MOVEMENT
> ALERTNESS . . . ALL THE TIME . . .

I HAVE to develop an "I'm invincible" mindset so I can keep going on even WITHOUT . . .

> FOOD
> AIR
> MOVE
> ALERTNESS
> (choice . . .) or else I'll die . . .

In addition to the normal adolescent feeling of "invincible" RAD carries that illusion to a whole new level for ALL of life . . . as a child . . . as a teen . . . and as an adult . . . what other options do I have? Die . . . and my MO is "don't die." And a HUGE crisis brews when the person is finally faced - like in their 50's - with the reality (that they can't rationalize or deny away anymore) that they are MORTAL!

UGG!

NOOOO!

* My instinct says it's wrong to die . . . the rest of me says it's hell to not die . . . what do I do?

NUMB – exist as little as possible . . . and feel as

little as possible . . .

AND . . .

WAIT for the day I don't have to do this anymore . . . and wait . . .

and wait . . .

and wait . . .

and wait . . .

* I'm writing this as if I want somebody to get it . . . to understand . . . but I believe that the only person who can truly "know it" . . . is another RAD person – and they don't need me to explain it to them . . . because they've been living it (whether they know the name for it or not)! I really don't want non-RAD people to truly understand – experientially – what RAD is like . . . I don't wish this on anyone at all . . . ever . . . but at least to understand they can't totally understand it . . . maybe that's where I'm going with this. As soon as they try to put this into some diagnostic code or category or tell me "I see" they've discounted what it really is ! !

RAD
     CAN'T
          FIT
               INTO WORDS . . .

And yet ... there's a part of me that wants Sandy to get it just because she's a therapist and she's supposed to get it. But I haven't wanted to show her what I'm writing. Don't know if I'll ever show her.

I just realized that I've been thinking I needed to put all this down in a sequence or in a logical manner that would flow and make sense to somebody else. The truth is, RAD isn't sequential or logical – not really – I mean the "logic" behind ALL thinking / behavior is the MO **"The only person I trust in this whole world to look out for me is me."** From that point on, I do whatever I need to do right then to "not die." There is no true sequence or logic inside. What RAD feels is the exact same as this I'm writing down – jumbled
> random
> from point to point
> hurried and messy
> hastily written down . . .

And yet . . . everything I do feels calculated and thought out tactically . . . so I don't get hurt again . . .
It's crazy . . .

That's what my brain is like ALL the time!

> THAT'S why I'm so
> easily sensory
> overloaded . . .

that's why I don't like to have to
    "think on my feet" – if I can
        avoid it. That's why I'm
            easily distracted . . .

NO WONDER my grade school
teachers said I was never paying
attention in class. Who cares what 2 + 2
equals when I'm just trying to "not die"??
But they thought it was just me being
disobedient and uncooperative. I do
remember that part. Go figure . . . but
. . . I guess they didn't know and
couldn't have known anyway . . .
Oh well . . .

That's also why I work so HARD to keep
things simple and organized. That's why
I want time to "process" and try to create
some internal logic, sequence . . .

        ORDER . . .
        CONTROL . . .

THAT'S what I'm trying to achieve . . .

Because ORDER + CONTROL = NOT GET
HURT!!

OK . . . having just said I try to keep
things "organized" . . . I also use clutter

and disorganization as camouflage to hide in . . .

Yet another contradiction . . .

* RAD =

Terror + **RAGE** +

Sleep problems + Depression +

PTSD + Terror + OCD +

Terror + Isolation /Aloneness +

PAIN + TRAUMA +

Numb + PAIN + NO TRUST +

TERROR + Fatigue issues + etc. . . . .

* One of my many SURVIVAL tactics was to NOT STAND OUT. I knew deep down inside that I didn't FIT IN because of the military brat thing (which they now call "TCK" or "Third Culture Kid") . . . @ least - to survive - I didn't want to STICK OUT and make myself an easy target . . . so camouflage . . . blend in . . . keep your head low and keep moving.

Other "tactics" -
    Avoid
    Withdraw - basically stay away
        from people
    Eat the loss myself - take the
        "hit" and move on
    Be anonymous (hide)
    Don't share personal things
        about myself
    Dump them before they dump me
    "I can take it" . . . the invincible
        thinking thing
    Never trust - don't know how to
        even if I wanted to . . .
    Not depend on anyone (really).

Sometimes I have to pretend to depend on another person in order to "blend in."
    So I pretend

Not to want anything. It will only
      lead to disappointment which =
      hurt
Not to need anything really
      because I won't get it anyway
Not feel, because the only thing I'll
      feel is PAIN!
Always check and double-check it
      MYSELF
"Look" as normal as I can
Do it my way or don't do it at all
"Wait out the storm"/endure longer
      than anyone else
Do it myself
Don't ask for assistance – goes
      along with "do it myself"
Don't believe what people say
Get it over with ASAP – so it can be
      a "for sure" thing . . . finally
"Trust" only memories because even
      things can be taken away from
      me
– don't attach to ANYTHING . . .
                     ANYONE . . .
                     EVER . . .
Either be in charge or don't be
      present at all
ALWAYS be able to move . . . run . . .
      ALWAYS . . .
Stockpile food (especially goodies)
      whenever I can

Try to do everything perfectly – so I
won't get in trouble = hurt
Scope things out so I know what to
do before I have to do it
Sit with my back to the wall not
toward the middle of the room
– so nobody can sneak up
behind me and strangle me
Keep the body toughened up so it
won't get soft – punish it . . .
make it hurt just to keep it in
shape
Shoot first and don't bother to ask
questions later
Get there early and "scope out" the
place first
Always know where the nearest exit
is – sit close to one if I can
EVERY decision/chore/action is
HUGE because that may be the 1
time something goes wrong and
somebody will get hurt
ALWAYS take SUPER good care of
something I have because it has
to "last forever" because I'll
never be able to get another one
. . . EVER

Winning is the only option
Always be aware of what's behind you

Dissociate
    Levels (Mild) = Avoid/ignore
                        Numb
                        Disconnect
                        Dissociate/repress
            (Severe) = Not logged in
                        memory at all
    All levels are tactics . . .
            depending on the "need"
            level
    Never confess or admit to
            anything

Almost all of the "tactics" have an "AL-WAYS" or "NEVER" as the key part of them. They make up a collection of tactics/thinking patterns that are the ROE = "Rules Of Engagement" I live by.

One SUPREME TACTIC is =

NEVER, under any circumstances, waver

From the ROE ! NEVER! . . .
EVER . . .

This is where the perfectionistic "SHOULD" and "SHOULDN'T" thinking comes into play.

Because . . .
      if I do all the SHOULDS
      ("ALWAYS")

      AND

      if I don't do the SHOULDN'TS
      ("NEVER")

      then . . .

   I won't get hurt = I won't die.

So the perfectionistic thinking is not because of simply trying to be "perfect" . . . it's to NOT GET HURT = NOT DIE! . . .

Here's where some of the OCD (Obsessive Compulsive Disorder) patterns can come into play (or more accurately, OCPD; Obsessive Compulsive Personality Disorder) so as to be SURE I ALWAYS follow the ROE . . .
      ALWAYS . . .
               ALWAYS . . .

The ROE could easily have 65 volumes to it with thousands of specific tactics in each volume!! No wonder it's hard to concentrate on anything else! Really

Because . . . if I break any
rule in the ROE . . .

I will DIE ! ! !

I don't really want to die . . .

so . . .

keep the ROE always
before me and
ALWAYS
do just as it says

ALWAYS . . .

* More "tactics" of mine =

Think and rethink . . . and keep
thinking . . .
Stay "lean and mean" physically
NEVER make a mistake – because
this may be the 1 mistake that
costs me my life
Find the other person's weak spot.
You never know when you will
need to exploit it

* My mind had a hard time shutting off
last night because it was being

flooded with thoughts of what to put down. Along with all the thoughts was the "write it down NOW or it will forever be
forgotten!" I had to get up and make some notes to @ least remind me of what I wanted to write this morning. Otherwise I wouldn't have gotten any sleep at all. YUCK ! ! UGGGGGH . . .

* That "NOW – or NEVER" feeling is all too familiar. That's the panicky feeling of RAD . . . "NOW! Or it's NEVER! . . .
                    EVER . . .
                        EVER . . .
                            EVER . . . !"

* Other similar "mottos" –

    "Last man standing"
    "Life's a b**** . . . then you die"
    "You snooze . . . you lose"

It's not anything personal – that's LIFE. Everybody knows that. "Last man standing" is nothing personal against you – it's that it's gonna be me . . . because my MO is "NOT DIE!" The "you snooze . . . you lose" is not personal either . . . that's just the way the world really does operate = "1st come . . . 1st serve."

THAT'S NORMAL and I see everyone as either living that way - or needing (if they're smart) - to live that way.

* The 65 volumes of the ROE I was talking about before . . . there's no page numbers, no categories, no filing system for the tactics . . . no table of contents either. Each tactic got written down in the heat of the moment and scratched out on any open space I could find @ that particular instant. No index either . . . no anything . . . In some cases I guess a RAD person (not me though) could separate the ALWAYS and the NEVERS into separate volumes . . . but the volumes aren't in any sequence or order - they're stacked up randomly on the floor inside my brain. Soooooo, that's the way the ROE thinking is set up . . .

BUT . . .
    AND . . .
        BUT . . .
            AND . . .

And there's a self-punishing action/ mechanism that will attack me if I EVER break - or attempt to break - the ROE!

- "You know better, Stupid!"

- "Don't EVER break the rules!"
- "How can you be soooooo stupid?!"
- "Don't EVER again EVEN THINK of
  not following the ROE!"

Does any of this chaos make sense? No
organization to the ROE volumes BUT . . .
AND . . . if I don't follow the rules –
EXACTLY, PERFECTLY . . . I'll be
punished

> by the world
> or by myself.

So . . . living in a constant state of
> SHOCK . . .
> NUMB . . .
> TERROR . . .

> there's the
> <u>added</u>
> "worry" of
> self-punishment
> if I break the
> rules. So in a
> sense . . .

EVERYBODY <u>IS</u> out to get me – even me!

* Surviving = the suffering continues
. . . and continues . . . and continues
. . . and continues . . . Can't suicide – it's

against the MO ("DON"T DIE!") . . . and all the ROEs are in place to make sure the MO is met . . .

   BUT . . .

     if I get kidnapped by a crazy man and killed or get killed on my motorcycle . . . then my life was "taken from me" and I "went down fighting" but still got to stop living anymore . . .

I have an alibi so I won't be punished for breaking the ROE . . . But I still get to stop surviving = stop the suffering . . .

     FINALLY . . .

That why there's often a "death wish" sort of thing a RAD person has . . . SOOOO many things are contradictions inside the brain. So many things pulling in opposite directions @ the same time . . .

SO MANY PARADOX s

to try to keep straight amid all the chaos . . . and the rain . . . and the darkness . . . and the jungle vegetation

. . . and the firefight . . .

And that fuels the NEED to have things
BLACK vs WHITE
RIGHT vs WRONG
ALL or NOTHING
FRIEND or FOE

Because there's no TIME to sort through
everything and come to a "logical"
conclusion . . . it's "NOW OR DEAD." I
have 0.00002 seconds to act in order to
save my life and not die . . . So "life" HAS
to be BIONARY . . . with only 2
"options" . . .

* There is no TIME . . . really . . . it's all
reactionary . . . instinct . . . It's a honed
skill vets have perfected – the ones who
didn't perfect it, are dead . . .
oh well . . .

* I saw this somewhere and simplified it
down for my brain to understand. It's
based on the Object Relations/Attachment
work by two authors Bowlby and
Ainsworth[5].

"The Attachment Behavioral System"

2 Sets of "core beliefs"
1. From SELF dimension
   "Am I worthy of being loved?"
   "Am I competent to get the love I need?"
2. From OTHER dimension
   "Are others reliable and trustworthy?"
   "Are others accessible and willing to
   respond to me when I need them?"

SECURE ATTACHMENT STYLE	AVOIDANT ATTACHMENT STYLE
Positive SELF Positive OTHERS	Positive SELF Negative OTHERS
"I'm OK . . . You're OK."	"I'm OK . . .You're not OK."
"I AM worthy of being loved . AND . . . you ARE able to give me the love I need."	"I AM worthy of being loved . . . BUT . . . you ARE NOT able to give me the love I need."

AMBIVALENT ATTACHMENT STYLE	**DISORGANIZED ATTACHMENT STYLE**
Negative SELF Positive OTHERS	Negative SELF Negative OTHERS
"I'm not OK . . . You're OK."	"I'm not OK . . . You're not OK."
"I'm NOT worthy of being loved	"I'm NOT worthy of being loved
AND . . . you ARE able to give me the love I need but DON'T because I'm unworthy of love."	AND . . . you ARE NOT able to give me the love I need I'm not Worthy of love anyway."

SECURE ATTACHMENT

The secure infant attaches because the "5-point criteria" for attachment has been met:

1. Seeks proximity, or closeness, to the caregiver, especially in times of trouble
2. Sees the caregiver as providing a "safe haven"
3. Trusts the caregiver to provide a secure base from which to explore the world
4. Feels fear/anxiety at the threat of separation from the caregiver
5. Feels grief and sorrow at the loss of the caregiver

AVOIDANT ATTACHMENT

The avoidant attachment child/person often struggles with at least 1 of the following:

1. Emotional connectedness
2. Disclosure of private thoughts and feelings
3. Non-sexual touch

"Others are not reliable to meet my needs, so I must rely on myself alone to meet my needs."

3 "Shades of Avoidance": (1) Narcissistic self, (2) Disconnected self, (3) Compulsive perfectionist self

The avoidant attachment child/person tends to keep people at a distance, avoid true intimacy and values success and power over relationships.

AMBIVALENT ATTACHMENT

The key issue is: dependency because of fear of abandonment

Parenting styles likely to produce ambivalent attachment in a child:
1. The cold-shoulder treatment
2. Overprotection
3. Withholding affection and approval
4. "Invisible fences" (i.e. not knowing where the boundaries really are)

3 "Shades of Dependency": (1) Anxious self, (2) Melodramatic self, (3) Angry self

The ambivalent attachment child person becomes entangled in relationships, with "come close – stay away" patterns and excessive concerns about rejection and abandonment.

DISORGANIZED ATTACHMENT

Dissociation is a normal response in disorganized attachment

The disorganized child person often bounces back and forth between avoidant and ambivalent attachment patterns

Effects of disorganized attachment style:
1. Identity problems
2. Emotional "stones" (5 common triggers of emotional "stones"): (1) Relationship disputes, (2) Transitions, (3) Unresolved grief, (4) Loneliness, (5) Negative thinking
3. Physical arousal (hyper-arousal)
4. Identification with the aggressor abuser (traumatic bonding)
5. Faulty assumptions (irrational thinking)
6. Distress relationships such as: (1) Faulty selection, (2) Distortion or (3) Provocation

Well . . . this sure shows me a lot! OUCH!

The "disorganized attachment" style sounds like me . . . 5 out of 6 effects . . . everything but the "identifying with the aggressor" one . . .

* OK . . . so I see where I fit on the chart . . . but what's to do about it all ? ? ?

* So . . . the dissociation is not a coping skill for ALL RAD people? Hummmm . . . I would have through it would be. Guess not . . . just the "disorganized" types like me have that going on . . .

BUT IT MAKES PERFECT SENSE TO ME . . .

DAHA ! ! If you can't physically get away from the whatever . . . you disconnect mentally to "get away" on the inside = dissociation . . .
AND IT WORKS ! ! ! Yeah it does . . .

I HATE THIS ! ! !

* RAD people ABSOLUTELY believe they are UNLOVABLE . . . and we can PROVE it . . .

OK . . . I'm going crazy here . . . in that last entry, I used "they" which is 3rd person and "we" . . . 2nd person (I think) both in the same sentence when I'm talking about ME (1st person). Wow . . . How crazy is that ? ?
    NO . . .
    How DISCONNECTED is THAT !!!!

AUGGAGG!!

That was stupid . . . now . . . where was I . . . oh yea . . . we believe we're totally unlovable and we can prove it . . .

    Well . . . because if I WAS "lovable" I would not have been treated this way! !

    Hello ! !

You don't treat things that are lovable, important and valuable to you badly . . .

And . . . since I WAS treated badly . . . that
PROVES I'm not.

What else am I – especially as a child – to conclude ? ?
You tell me? What other conclusion is any child going to draw when treated that way?

The kid HAS no other options . . . it's "I'm totally unlovable". . . that's it. . .

That's the "final answer" . . . and it's all PRE-COGNITIVE too . . . so the kid can't go back later and re-think themselves out of it.

IT JUST IS THE WAY IT IS . . . Like fish in water and the sun raising in the East . . . It's not up for debate. Nobody debates that the sun comes up in the East . . . it would be STUPID to argue that . . . we all KNOW that's the way it is . . .

That's how this is too. It just IS. "I'm unlovable" . . . and there's no discussion. I don't know how to explain it . . . IT JUST IS . . .

AND I JUST <u>AM</u> . . . UNLOVABLE that is . . .

PERIOD

* I think this makes sense as to why such a varying degree of reactions/behaviors in RAD . . .

RAD + INTEROVERTED person =
Camouflage = hide, stay low, evade, have your M16 and grenades at the ready — but don't use them b/c that compromises your position.
Introverted people tend to soak things IN with not much coming back OUT . . . as a general rule:

. . . avoid . . . avoid . . . avoid . . .

But . . . if you corner or surprise me . . . you'll get the full fury of my M16, grenades and all the booby traps I've set up around me. That's when it's fight to the death and I go for the kill shot first thing. It's not "personal" . . . that's just how it is in the jungle war. People take things sooooooo personally . . . I don't get that AT ALL . . .

RAD + EXTROVERTED person = Run through the jungle firing at anything that even looks like it's moving and throwing grenades at anything that remotely appears to be a threat and don't even look back.

Because extroverted people tend to be focused OUTWARD, as a general rule, and whatever is going on INSIDE tends to come OUT as it's going on inside. "What you see is what you get" sort of thing.

The "war" is coming OUT in "real time" just as it's being played out internally . . . every moment . . . every scenario . . . every part of everything . . . attack . . . attack . . . attack . . .

Me . . . I'm the introverted type of person . . . just leave me alone and all will be fine . . .

That's all I can remember as a child – what little I CAN remember – wanting . . .

Just to be left alone . . . It's when people did NOT leave me alone that everything broke loose . . .

LEAVE

ME

ALONE

That's all I ever wanted in life . . . life would be better for me AND for everyone if they'd just leave me alone

But people DON'T just leave others alone . . .

WHY? Just live and let live. How can it be that hard??

I never started any of the fights in school . . . it's only when some guy would do something stupid . . . and keep bugging me and keep it up . . . is when I'd unleash on him . . . just to make him LEAVE ME ALONE !

I can't understand why the world just can't leave people to themselves !

Whenever Father would be around the house he was into my business - trying to be the "good father" and do the order me around thing. But it only bugged me.

Whenever Mother did pay any attention to me it was always about something I was doing that she didn't like - mostly because she thought it would make her look bad - nag . . . nag . . . nag . . .

Teachers all through school wouldn't just let me do my work the way I could do it best.

My ex-wife wouldn't let me be. She was always trying to "fix" me by telling me what to do and how to do it and dragging me to this social thing and that social thing. Sheeze!

Just . . .
leave me . . .
alone . . .

I will be better off. . . and believe me. . . YOU will be better off too . . .

That's NOT a hard concept . . . but people just don't get it . . .

Because . . . when you DO leave me alone in my camo or to wander around quietly . . . I WON'T BLOW UP ON YOU !

It's only when people press me . . . bother me . . . get in my space . . . push me or . . . try to "MAKE ME" (oooooh . . . that's a statement you NEVER make to a RAD person. Don't EVER go there.) that they make me blow up at them . . . Not because I hate them . . . I just want them to LEAVE ME THE HECK ALONE and they didn't listen when I said it nicely . . .

UGGGGGGGGGH!

What I truly do NOT understand is why people try to even deal with a RAD + EXTROVERT. Now THAT doesn't make any sense because as soon as you get close to them in any way you have a 90% chance of crossing them . . . defined as "doing something wrong according to their way of thinking" . . . and they'll shoot or throw a grenade at you . . . and sometimes even if you didn't do anything "wrong" they will STILL attack . . . because you made a leaf move in the jungle and they shoot everything that moves . . . or . . . just to keep you off balance . . . or just to make you hurt like they hurt inside . . . or just for the sake of feeling the power rush of manipulating, controlling or hurting you . . .

Anyway . . . again, trying to keep this whole thing objective and I just can't seem to do that. Stupid! I should be able to do that easily . . . UGGGGGGH . . .

Oh well . . . nobody is going to ever see this anyway . . . nor would I show it to anyone because they'd think I was crazy or something . . . or a serial killer or something like that . . .

It's simple . . . LEAVE ME ALONE . . .
and all will be well . . .

CONTROL = "Not Die" (the MO)
NO CONTROL = DIE ! ! Or . . .
at best = HURT ! !

(oops. Didn't mean to skip a page. Stupid.)

and it's ALL the control or NONE at all . . .

Control cannot be shared – it's "I have it ALL or . . .

I have NOTHING" . . . It's back to the

> BLACK vs. WHITE
> RIGHT vs. WRONG
> ALL or NOTHING
> FRIEND or FOE
> 1s or 0s

That's why any authority figure is an automatic threat:

> Parent
> Boss
> Therapist
> Teacher
> Police officer
> Pastor
> Leader
> Etc., etc., etc.
> Baby sitter
> Etc, etc., etc.

And remember, there's at least 2 ways to fight:
1. attack = shoot my M16 and throw grenades
2. avoid = hide in my camouflage and set booby traps

* There are many people who have no sense of rhythm at all. They just CANNOT ever clap or step or dance "to the beat" no matter how hard they try or how desperately they WANT to . . .

They just can't "find" the beat – rhythm – in them to match.

It's just NOT THERE . . .

A person with RAD is such a person as that . . . I just CANNOT find the cadence . . . the beat . . . the rhythm that will get me "in sync" with another person (not really) . . . no matter how hard I try or now desperately I WANT to. I just can't FIND the "sync" – the rhythm – to connect w/ another person . . . Not really . . . It's NOT a choice . . . it's NOT a simple matter of "learning how to . . ."

IT'S NOT HERE !

And I have come to the painful awareness that it's NOT here and that it never WILL BE HERE . . .

I don't have what everybody else has . . . and that makes me feel even MORE isolated . . . and ALONE . . .

I've given up trying to "clap along" . . .

> or "join the dance" . . .

>> or "fall in step" . . . as all the clichés go.

* I can see why a RAD person would want/choose to join a gang . . . or the Marines . . . or want to be a part of a Special Forces team . . . because while they can NOT attach to another PERSON . . . they may be able to attach to a GROUP . . .
an IDEA . . .
a MISSION . . .
a PHILOSOPHY . . .
a PURPOSE . . .

All these things are a "someTHING" . . . not a "someONE" . . . A someTHING will never leave them . . . reject them . . . abandon them . . . The someTHING is a THING not a PERSON. The someTHING is a THING that can't EVER be taken away from them . . . even if they were "once" a part of it . . . or "once" a member of it . . . or "once" went there . . .

Not much different than the statement: "There's no such thing as an ex-Marine."

It's a someTHING that will last FOREVER . . . it IS SAFE

It IS SECURE . . . It IS a BELONGING (even if it's in the past) that is either real or an illusion or both . . . that goes beyond a frail human connection (breakable and insecure — at least in the RAD person's mind) . . .

> A BELONGING that I can HOLD on to

> FOREVER . . .

> FINALLY . . .

> (relief !)

That's why a gang member is willing to DIE for "the GANG" . . . or "the COLORS" . . . or "the CREED" . . . or "the PATCH" . . . All are the someTHING that is NOT a person – another individual member – but BIGGER than them (the person or people) and will continue on even without the "them" (the persons).

* OK . . . some other things about how RAD thinks. How I "define" the word FAMILY . . .

This won't make any sense but "family" is anybody I'm with right now and wherever I am right now. "Home is where your rump rests."

And the word CAREGIVER . . . don't really even understand that word really . . . but a "caregiver" is . . .

Anybody I'm with right now who can give me what I want right now . . .

The weird thing about no attachment is I'll go with almost anybody if I think I can get what I want from them or where they are. It's not an "over attachment" it's just since there is no attachment at all, to anything or anyone, no one place is any worse than any other place . . . and besides, you may have ice cream at your house.

RAD has no *attachment* to an "actual" caregiver or to an "actual" family unit. Why do you think street kids can "bond" together with other kids they don't even know and make up a "family unit"?
DAHA ! ! !

RAD people can NOT feel (b/c they're disconnected):

>Love
>Guilt
>Empathy
>Need
>Not really . . . at least at first . . .

Again . . . if RAD is on that continuum thing (which makes sense to me) then these reactions/thinking patterns will likely be on a continuum as well . . . Only makes sense.

Back on track . . . where do things like "love . . . guilt . . . empathy . . . need" fit in a jungle war ! ? !
HELLO ! !

"All's fair in love and war" . . . and this is WAR . . . so . . . anything goes. It's not "personal" it's just the way the war/world IS . . . and besides if you TAKE TIME to

FEEL anything . . . especially –
    Love
    Guilt
    Empathy
    Needs . . .

            You'll get distracted
            and get your head
            blown off !! It's NOT
            that I WANT to be . . .

    UN-loving
    UN-guilt aware (not sure how to
    say this one)
    UN-empathic
    NOT need

THERE'S NO TIME or PLACE for any of
those things . . . It's kill or be killed . . .

    it's duck and hide . . .

            it's shoot first and don't
            even bother to ask
            questions later . . .

                it's keep moving . . .
                moving . . . moving . . .
                (you reload and eat
                on the run).

* Deciding on whether to show this to Sandy next apt. Don't know. Don't think so . . . We'll see . . .

* Weird but ROCKING MOTION is something very KEY with RAD people . . . not sure why . . .

I often rock myself . . . "sway" more like it . . . and that swaying motion just seems like it's a *have to* thing sometimes.

I remember being told I would not ever want to be held or "rocked" as a kid.

That would make sense now that I'm beginning to understand all this RAD stuff. If SOMEBODY ELSE is doing the holding and/or rocking . . .

> that means . . . THEY'RE IN CHARGE !

But . . . this makes sense now too . . . if I INITIATE the hug or holding . . . THEN it's OK . . .

> because . . . I'M IN CHARGE . . . and that's OK then.

I must have driven Mother crazy with the way I acted and responded to her. Must have driven any babysitter crazy too. Or maybe I was "great" to baby sit b/c I just stayed under my camouflage and did my own thing and they got paid to do nothing but watch TV or whatever . . . The rhythmic motion of rocking is a soothing action. It's an attempt to self-comfort. And . . . it's ALL UP TO ME . . . to TAKE CARE OF ME . . .

RAD people don't develop "cooperative play" . . . or at least not very well . . .

Well . . . DAHA . . . there's no TIME or PLACE to "PLAY" in the jungle war . . . Not unless you want to DIE !

* I found out I tend to run 1 – 2 levels higher of stress hormones than "normal" people. My MD has been harping on that for some time now but can't figure out why.

It makes sense (how many times have I said that phrase so far . . . but things ARE beginning to FINALLY make sense . . . and that's a good thing because for so many years things DIDN'T make any sense.) that my stress hormones are higher because we're in a constant state of SHOCK and SURVIVAL and we NEED that adrenalin flowing through our system (even if it's "just in case").

But, according to my MD, adrenalin is a toxic substance and can (and does) work against the body if there's too much too often – which is ALL the time for me.

So now . . . the very hormone I'm using to attempt to SURVIVE and "not die" is also my enemy and will hurt me!

It's a "catch 22"
"Damned if I do . . .
      and damned if I don't."

So I'll choose to NOT DIE NOW because I don't even have the time to think about long range consequences. I think that's a lot of why I need to constantly move physically – to work out the adrenalin in my body somehow – give it somewhere to be used up so it won't poison me. The TWITCHY or constant movement thing is because of 2 things:

(1) anxiety/terror in the body

(2) large amounts of adrenalin that's not focused on any particular action at present.

And that hormone level becomes the "norm" for us RAD people. Like mountaineering on an extreme peak in extreme weather. You're sooooo tired you want to sit down and rest, but you don't let yourself . . . b/c if you sit down you'll fall asleep and you'll freeze to death as you sleep . . .

        so it's keep moving . . . one step at a time . . . step . . . step . . . step . . . with the MO of "don't die" ringing in your ears, there are NO OPTIONS . . . you step . . .
                step . . .
                    step . . .

THAT'S WHY the NUMB and DISSOCIATION are so NECESSARY. That's the only way you can keep going – separate the mind from the body . . .

"Divide and SURVIVE."

And the NUMB and DISSOCIATION WORK! It's intended to work . . .
        in emergencies . . .

but . . . that's the state RAD is in 24/7 stuck in SHOCK and SURVIVAL MODE.

STEP . . .
STEP . . .
STEP . . .

"Living" ("not dying") is hell even without feeling the body or emotions. Just imagine what it would be like if I did feel the body and emotions

NO ••• can't do that . . . It's too much and would overload the system and I'd self-destruct. "Divide and Survive" and DISSOCIATE is my lifesaver.

So is sleeping – it's an escape – a dissociation of sorts . . . but when I sleep my sleep is disturbed . . . So even my lifesaver has a price to be paid – it hurts me ! ! !

THERE'S NO SAFE PLACE . . . It's "survive at all costs" . . .

and . . .

> survive = suffering more and more and longer and longer

That's why "Life's a b****, then you die."

Some of us get to die sooner than the rest.

> They're the lucky ones . . . b/c they don't have to suffer anymore.

I know that's opposite of the typical American mindset that says "You're lucky to have made it through."

WRONG . . .

No wonder why RAD people have a hard time with things like:

> Remembering things
> Concentration
> Learning things the 1st time
> Paying attention
> Socializing

RAD "FORMULA"

INSIDE = all of this stuff I've written down so far
+ (PLUS)

OUTSIDE = the jungle war, night time, rainstorm, fire fight, etc., etc., etc.

= (EQUALS)

A hell of a life!

The lucky ones are the ones who died in the trauma. They didn't suffer anymore. It's over for them. I'm glad for them. I envy them too. Wish it were me.

I don't know where all of this is going – if anywhere – yet it seems important – at least for me – to write as much of this out as I can. I have started asking professionals I know . . . when I can sneak it in . . . about RAD and try to put everything I hear down on paper here. Maybe some day it will make sense or I can organize it somehow . . .

So . . . how did I make ANY connection w/ my ex and son at all? I know it was w/ my son first . . . maybe b/c he wasn't

a threat to me . . . at least not as a child
. . .

People use the phrase "God's grace" so
flippantly . . . I think in my case I really
do believe it was by God's grace only
that I had any connection to either of
them . . . even though he's not speaking
to me now . . .

As I look at all of this now, I'm so sad
for her and what she had to live w/
being married to me – a RAD spouse.

> It wasn't fair to her . . . and she got
> hurt . . .
>> all because of ME . . .

* Homework assignment: Define what I
think the word "safe" means. I can't use
the dictionary, just answer it myself.

> I'm drawing a B I G blank . . .

Thinking that "SAFE" does NOT EXIST . . .
anywhere . . . There is no SAFE PLACE . . .
REALLY . . . in the jungle war . . .

Ok . . . here's my answer for Sandy next
session:

S = sufficiently
A = away
F = from
E = everyone

NO SAFE + SURVIVE = SUFFER . . . I don't want to suffer anymore.

So . . . I guess I'll have to figure out how to NON-EXIST (can't break the MO of "not die". . . but maybe I can "non-exist."

SAFE means NO PAIN . . . AT ALL . . .
EVER . . .
NEVER AGAIN . . .
NOT EVEN A
LITTLE BIT.

NO PAIN!
(anymore!)

Where in this world can you be guaranteed of "no pain whatsoever", at all, ever, no how, no way? THERE IS NO PLACE that can guarantee that . . . SO > > >

I can NEVER be safe . . . SAFE does NOT even EXIST . . .

It's SURVIVE at all costs ("NOT DIE")

AND . . .

keep / stay / get away from the
PAIN as much as I can – all the
time – no matter what . . .

RUN ! ! ! !

PAIN = "Being destroyed !"

Because . . .

As a small child things like:
rejection, abandonment, un-safe
routine, safety (physically,
emotionally or sexually) DO have the
power to DESTROY . . . physically . . .
emotionally . . . even spiritually . . .

So . . . ALL pain becomes pain that will
DESTROY . . .

But . . .

According to Sandy, there are
really 2 kinds / styles of PAIN:

(1) PAIN that just hurts because it
hurts because it hurts, BUT it won't
DESTROY me – like running a

marathon. It will hurt – your lungs will burn, your heart will pound mercilessly and your legs will become enflamed in pain . . . hurt . . . hurt . . . hurt . . . BUT . . . THERE'S NO "DESTRUCTION" GOING ON to the body. When you stop . . . the pain subsides and settles out and there's no "DAMAGE."

(2) PAIN that DOES mean "DESTRUCTION" of some sort (physically, emotionally, spiritually, etc.). Like when I broke my thumb and I tried to lift weights the next day – b/c I didn't really think "anything was wrong." BUT . . . the more I tried to lift . . . the more it hurt . . . because it WAS CAUSING DAMAGE to the tissue, ligaments, etc. all around the thumb to keep lifting. Daha . . .
She said for RAD both (1) and (2) kinds of pain get welded together and become the SAME:
BOTH feel like they will DESTROY
BOTH FEEL like they need to be avoided AT ALL COST
BOTH feel like they will "kill."

Part of the healing journey, she says, has to do with redefining "PAIN" into the 2 categories it actually is . . . to UN-weld the two and then consciously work at separating them in my mind and body time and time again. NOT an easy task.

It NEEDS to be done – the separating of the 2 kinds of pain – if the RAD person is going to be able to redefine "SAFE" and "TRUST" . . . because . . . in this life there WILL BE PAIN; (1) kind. One of the hardest new thinking patterns for me to grasp has been "I can feel pain (#1 kind) AND STILL BE SAFE . . . BOTH . . .

Realize PAIN (2) still needs to be STOPPED or RUN AWAY from! There are STILL things, people; circumstances that want to/try to DESTROY me . . .

> BUT (and this is a VERY BIG "BUT") . . .
>
> not EVERY thing or EVERY person or EVERY circumstance . . .

There are SOME things, people, circumstances that are NOT out to DESTROY me.

> still SOME . . . but not ALL.
>
> And . . . I can feel PAIN (#1

kind) . . . (not that I "like" it) . . .

AND . . .

STILL BE SAFE too . . .

* Not sure about all she's suggesting.

BUT my definition of SAFE has to change too. SAFE will need to acknowledge that the #1 kind of PAIN exists but will NOT destroy . . . and it can COEXIST with SAFE . . .

THAT is a VERY . . . VERY HARD truth for RAD to buy into ! ! !

But . . . it IS the TRUTH . . .
and the TRUTH will set me FREE . . .

(Someday – sooner than
later I hope.)

BUT (soooooo many contradictions)
. . . the body – being an expert @ being
NUMB/DISSOCIATED . . .

does NOT know HOW to evaluate PAIN . . .

KENISTETICALLY all pain is the same and is to be AVOIDED @ ALL COSTS . . .

So to begin to "feel" the body is a HUGE RISK –

This is totally crazy . . . being willing to feel at all . . . much less the BODY . . . for goodness sake!

AUGGGGGG GGG

Too big of a RISK !

ALL HEALING along the RAD journey is RISK after RISK after RISK . . .

And you have to understand just HOW BIG OF A RISK IT TRULY IS. It feels like a LIFE & DEATH risk –

> ALL or NOTHING
> DO or DIE

And the RISK is taking me into the unknown = can't control it = might get HURT = DIE . . .

"NO! Don't take the risk !!
Stay where you are. There's
less to lose by staying with
the suffering you know so
well . . .

DON'T RISK !"

REMEMBER – the ROE is what has kept
me alive all these years – that's the
belief I've had to maintain – so why
would I EVER go AGAINST the rules that
have kept me from dying? ? ? Dying is
NOT worth the risk – ANY RISK.

MO = "Don't die!"

That's why I have – HAVE – to understand
(a sense of control) the risk in front of
me and I have – HAVE – to see the
possible/probable advantage if I "leap"
. . . I also need the freedom NOT to risk
– or at least – not yet.

Remember – so many of the ROE and
cognitive thinking patterns were written
in blood and terror. They are charged
with energy/power. ANY risk against
that energy is risky in and of itself
because there's the "self-punishment"
safety mechanism inside that is designed

to keep me from going against that ROE energy/power. I can self-mutilate, self-sabotage . . . even participate in self-destruction and it's all an attempt to keep me IN LINE with the ROE . . . which is an attempt to keep me ALIVE – NOT DIE.

That's why I don't see teenagers – at least me when I was a teen – being able to come out of RAD. They don't have the ego strength, the solidness, to fight this kind of fight – yet. The internal ROE and safety mechanisms are working fine and TOO GOOD to be over ridden – yet.

I don't see it happening at all . . . not really . . . Can SOME "healing" progress be made = maybe . . . but complete healing for RAD = no.

And that's ANOTHER thing. The therapist that came up with that holding theory had NO CLUE of how RAD really thinks and operates! It does NOT cause the child to become attached or dependent – NEVER ! ! !

> ALL it does is:
> > creates traumatic bonding (not
> > > healthy bonding)

creates deeper dissociation
creates splits in the personality
     (to give the "adult"
       whatever they eventually
       want in the way they think
       it's suppose to look like)
reinforces the RAD MO and
forces a whole bunch of new
rules to be added to the ROE

IT DOES NOT/CANNOT HELP . . . AT ALL!

EVER . . .

REALLY . . .

Glad they stopped using that "technique."
STUPID ! !
You see, the RAD world/thinking is:

    BLACK or WHITE
      DO or DIE
    FRIEND or FOE
    ALWAYS or NEVER

So it makes sense that BEHAVIOR patterns
will be "polarized" and at times, flip-flop
back and forth between those 2
polarized opposites:

Fight	Flight
Rebellious, defiant Resisting any and all authority	"Go with the flow" Stockholm Syndrome or traumatic bonding
Bullying or abusing others	Overly kind - trying to "rescue" others
Be the "life of the party"	Avoid the party all together
Sexually active or promiscuous	Sexually "neutral" or "a-sexual"
Go home with anyone	Avoid everyone at all times
Binge/hoard food	Restrict food (to keep from "needing" it)
Not let anyone "hurt" me	Yet OK to "hurt" myself
Don't care at all	Try hard to look like I care
Draw attention to myself	Avoid all attention to myself at all times
"Don't Die"	"Don't want to keep going"
Control by force	Control by being the victim

Man . . . I didn't know there were so many polarizations going on inside. No wonder it feels so crazy inside!

No wonder it's safer NOT to feel – b/c I can't feel the "crazy" then either . . .

Anyway . . . more polarizations:

Hurt others	Try to "rescue" others
OVERT show of power	COVERT use of power (passive-aggressive)
Aim RAGE at SELF (inside)	Aim RAGE at OTHERS (outside)
No boundaries	No "touch" at all
Back	Forth
Up	Down
Over	and Over
Back	and Forth

Because THERE'S NO TIME to sort things out that may fall "in the middle" . . . Survival (= NO TIME) DEMANDS a binary world . . . You're EITHER "friend" OR you're FOE.

There no "neutral" in this war . . . because even "neutral" can cause PAIN/ HURT and is . . . therefore . . . an enemy = FOE

SHOULD   SHOULDN'T
Right   Wrong
Good   Bad
For me   Against me

RAD never had a chance to get out of the:

PAIN verses PLEASURE stage !!!

RAD is STILL stuck in the PAIN vs. PLEASURE part of the inner brain . . .
            But has to add to it because
            physically developing and
            growing demands a "FULLER"
            use of either/or terms –
            viewing things the same but with
            more "sophisticated" terms.

That's what makes the paradoxical

"schizophrenic" life of RAD.

That's how it is all the time every day of every week of every month of every year.

* I went back over my notes to see just how long I've been on this roller coaster . . . and it's been 3 years since this all began to unravel and 2 years of actual WORK to get out of all this. I had no idea of the time in all of this . . .

ALONE =

Feels safe (nobody around to hurt me)	Feels lonely and awful (nobody around to love me).

"You can take the soldier out of the war . . .

but . . . it's hard to take the war out of the soldier."

The healing process will need to look @ – and probably re-define:
Safe
Trust
Pain
Normal
"Ok"
Living

Friend
Rest
Possible verses probable
Possible verses present / now / real
. . . just a few of the concepts that will need to be rearranged inside the thinking and heart

"The first 2 days of a baby's EXTERNAL life . . . they decide whether the environment is SAFE or NOT." I have that phrase bouncing around inside my head. I heard it from somewhere. Maybe a radio show or something. If that's true . . . that's AMAZING !!

Hospitalization (for any reason) of an infant = HIGH STRESS

Because . . .

Medical care (procedures, needles, etc.) = PAIN = abuse = TRAUMA that NOBODY IS STOPPING !

RN shift staff changes (out of necessity of course) = multiple caregivers = changing faces and hands = NOBODY IS CONSTANT !

* The "familiar" mother's voice is NOT ALWAYS RIGHT THERE = abandoned by "mom" . . . b/c babies attach to the VOICE . . . then the FACE of the mother.

And none of this is anybody's fault. Nobody is neglectful so don't call out the attorneys. It just needs to be done medically for the infant's physical safety . . . but can (not always . . . but can . . .) traumatize the infant's emotional safety.

That's NOT FAIR ! ! It's NOT the infant's fault . . . it's NOT the mother's fault (unless she was a drug addict or did something to put her unborn baby in jeopardy) . . . it's NOT the medical profession's fault . . . BUT IT JUST HAPPENS ! ! UGGGGG !

NOT FAIR !

I read, or heard, that at five months of gestation the lymphatic system is in place and the amygdala (the "fire alarm system" of the brain) begins receiving stress signals.

All these things about the brain keep coming out of my internet searching lately. Or maybe it's just that I'm tuning into them because of all I'm thinking and trying to write about. Anyway . . .

Another phrase: "The stronger the attachment (and therefore a sense of SAFE/TRUST) the less likely a negative event will cause PTSD (Post Traumatic Stress Disorder) in a child."

Daha ! ! Don't need a psychology degree to figure that one out!

NO attachment = state of SHOCK (survival state) already

+

a "negative event" or trauma will only MAGNIFY the already state of SHOCK and WILL become PTSD.

That just makes sense to me. Daha . . .

So . . .

HEALTHY attachment = NO state of shock all the time

+

a "negative event" or trauma will most likely impact the person / child but in a "first time" style which the body and mind can adjust to after the initial SHOCK phase WEARS OFF . . . which it does in "normal" people.

That's obvious . . . at least to me . . .

I guess I'm wrong in thinking that the things that make sense to me make sense to every one. Just like, OK, things that make sense to them . . . often don't make any sense to me. I guess we really are from "2 different worlds" as they say.

I'm from the jungle war, where it's night time, raining and there's a firefight going on . . .

and . . .

they're from Normaltown, USA
which I'm not sure how to even
describe . . .

OK, kind of dense, but I think I finally
got that one. A little bit slow here.
Uggggggggg . . .

Baby WILL ATTACH to caregiver IF/WHEN:

> there is "enough" protection (SAFE)

> there is "enough" proximity of the
> caregiver (SAFE)

> there is "enough" predictability in the
> environment (SAFE).

Baby WILL NOT ATTACH to the caregiver
IF/ WHEN:

> there is NOT "enough" protection
>   (UN-SAFE)

> there is NOT "enough" proximity of
> the caregiver (UN-SAFE)

there is NOT "enough" predictability in the environment - sameness / routine / order, etc.
(UN-SAFE).

The key word here is ENOUGH for that BABY and its personality. It does NOT have to be perfect or 100% or totally complete . . . BUT IT DOES have to be ENOUGH for that child to feel safe enough to attach . . .

Another polarization:

MINIMIZING   CATASTROPHIZING

TERROR is the 1st & core emotion in RAD

2nd is RAGE

* If a trauma occurs in a child's life it's seen as (   ); because of the "connecting" . . .

the person I connected to . . . hurt
me

the person I connected to . . . did
not stop the hurt from hurting me . . .

THEREFORE . . .

the child's brain becomes
wired NOT TO CONNECT in order to
avoid any future trauma . . . or so it
reasons . . .

OK . . . more "brain stuff" from a
workshop Sandy attended[6]. When an
infant/child has a NEED the right
hemisphere of the brain gets "turned on"
> > > baby EXPRESSES the need > > >
caregiver MEETS the NEED and trust is
developed (this is the diagram she drew
out earlier for me and I copied it in
here).

When the right hemisphere "turns on" (or
"opens up") it then gives the left
hemisphere permission to "turn on"
("open up") too and begin a conscious
problem-solving process = "logical" and
sequential thinking can then begin.

LEFT HEMISPHERE	RIGHT HEMISPHERE
Develops 18-36 months	Develops 0-24 months
Activated by EQUILIBRIUM	Activated by NOVELTY or emotion
Verbal	Non-verbal
Logical and sequential "The trees"	Non-linear and "random" "The Forest" (the whole) *Dedicated to affect regulation *Connections to endocrine and nervous systems

BUT . . . if/when the right hemisphere is "shut down" ("closed up") because of trauma (and the emotional surge that accompanies that trauma) . . . the right hemisphere doesn't WORK/ACTIVATE . . .

and when the right hemisphere "closes up" it will not signal the left hemisphere to "open up" . . .

so the left hemisphere doesn't WORK/ ACTIVATE EITHER . . .

THEREFORE . . . the ONLY part of the brain that IS "WORKING" IS THE "SURVIVAL SYSTEM" IN THE AMYGDALA . . .

FIGHT or FLIGHT
Pain or Pleasure
Do or Die
Black or White
Right or Wrong
Friend or Foe
Shoot or Duck
All or Nothing

THAT'S why it takes a RAD person – even after their journey of healing 6x (+ or –) LONGER to do a task before they "get it" or "remember it" or it becomes a habit.

And . . . the left hemisphere (I wish there was an abbreviation for these things! Oh well.) naturally works 7x slower in a traumatic event than in a non-traumatic event.

There was lots more stuff from the workshop she shared, but these are the things that stood out to me – at least according to my own notes.

All of that makes sense . . . now . . .
That's why "don't panic" thinking has to be TRAINED INTO people who are:
Soldiers
Rock climbers
Fire fighters
Police officers

because . . . it's not "NATURAL" so it has to be TRAINED INTO the brain.

I remember learning the STOP acrostic:

S = stop
T = think
0 = observe
P = plan

THEN . . . you can ACT . . .

Read - or rather "skimmed" - a book called The Emotional Brain[7]. It all sort of ran together in my brain but the one over-arching idea I came away with was that if a trauma happens to a child under the age of 2 it really messes with that amygdala part of the brain and de-regulates it so much (like a faulty car alarm) the child/person always misperceives incoming stimulus and therefore is always activating the "fight or flight" response.

That's what I mean by ANY stimulus = PAIN = "destroy me" = FIGHT or FLIGHT.

Because ANY stimulus can be seen as (interpreted as) PAIN . . . or POTENTIAL

PAIN in a WORLD WHERE THERE IS NO SAFETY . . .

DAHA! ! ! !

Yet another polarization:

FULL ALERT (sensing EVERY-THING)	Same time the body goes NUMB (feels NOTHING)

Because of the chaos/disorganization of the EXTERNAL world of the child with RAD . . . their INTERNAL world becomes chaotic/ disorganized too.

Just like the organization of my writing ! Just like all – or at least most – of RAD.

And it's every moment . . .
every thought . . .
every thing . . .

THAT'S WHY ! ! ! !
And it's NOT just BAD THINGS/TRAUMA that hurt a child's brain. NEGLECT (the LACK of GOOD THINGS) can damage a child just as much . . . if not more than bad things happening.

Why? Oh man, let's see if I can put this down on the page.

With TRAUMA (a BAD thing HAPPENING to me) the brain rallies around – organizes itself around – "SURVIVING" . . . which the brain knows how to "make sense of" in a sense.

But with NEGLECT (a GOOD thing NOT HAPPENING to me) the infant's/child's brain can't "figure out" or "make sense" of why the NEGLECT / ABANDONMENT. There's nothing in the brain to organize around. How do you grab a hold of a void? How do you explain a "nothing?" The brain CAN'T . . .

ABSENCE is MORE disorganizing than TRAUMA[8].

Neglect/absence is the TRAUMATIC EVENT of

NOTHINGNESS . . . a VOID . . .

All of this TRAUMA – the PRESENSE of the BAD or the ABSENCE of the GOOD – not only "hurts" the brain but can do

DAMAGE to the brain. You bet it can ! !
I'll bet that's a huge part of why I fight
depression all the time. And why my
son fights depression too - since he was
raised by a RAD father.

OK . . . OK . . . OK . . . all these different
people can diagnose and describe the:

> "disorganization"
> "de-regulation"
> "chaos"
> "dissociation"
> - blah . . . blah . . . blah . . .

BUT WHAT THAT FEELS LIKE AND LIVES
LIKE CAN'T BE PUT INTO WORDS ! !

> IT'S WAY BEYOND "AWFUL"

> IT'S WAY BEYOND
> "UNIMAGINABLE"

I don't know if they can even imagine
- unless they are RAD too - just HOW
"disorganized' THAT
"disorganization" FEELS . . .

> AND THE TERROR

> that CHAOS/

DISORGANIZATION
causes at the core of a
person's being . . .
It's NOT = "I'm a fairly stable individual
(fairly "organized" inside) and 9-11 threw
me for a loop."
It's = "I'm in a jungle war . . . it's all
black out . . . it's raining . . . it's an all
out fire fight . . . I'm running for my
life b/c I'm all alone out here . . . and
it's ALWAYS been like this . . . ALWAYS
. . . ALWAYS . . . and THEN I get hit with
the 9-11 thing!"

IT'S TOO MUCH

ALWAYS TOO MUCH

TOO MUCH . . .

An old saying says "The deepest expression of any emotion is silence." Because the reality of that emotion at its depth will go beyond what words can express or describe or capture.

Words at some point come to an end . . . but the emotion doesn't.

THAT'S SOOOOOOO TRUE WITH RAD ! ! !

I saw a documentary the other day on TV about the Vietnam War. One problem with using Vietnam (a jungle war) as a word picture for RAD is that in the real Vietnam soldiers had each other and at least the whole world knew what was going on. Other people understood it existed. They may have no idea what the soldier on the ground experienced or how it felt to be there . . . but at least they understood it was happening.

With RAD, it's a war ONLY I know of, ONLY I live in it and I am ALL ALONE in it. I'm fighting ALL ALONE . . . ALWAYS . . . and nobody else can "understand" that the war is even going on . . . much less understand what it's like to be IN the war.

> Except another RAD . . . then words aren't really needed . . .
>
> Just a look says it all
>
> A nod answers back fully . . .

SILENCE . . .

BUT . . . I STILL DON'T TRUST YOU . . . Even if you DO understand the RAD stuff b/c you're RAD yourself . . . you are STILL seen as a FOE . . . because EVERYBODY is a FOE . . . and you're part of the "everybody" . . . and besides . . . you may be even more of a threat b/c you know your way around the jungle better than all those civilian people. So meeting another RAD person – even if we did admit it to each other – is NOT SAFE. Well, let me back up here. It can be "OK" IF/WHEN there's been enough healing in both so that they can feel a bit SAFE and feel safe enough to even admit this to another human being. Because if I were to tell another person all this is going on inside my head all the time . . . they would think I'm crazy and have me committed!

So if 2 RAD people are far enough along in their healing . . . then maybe they COULD meet up and get the rest of the way out of this jungle by helping each other . . . and walking together . . . Just maybe . . .

And that right there is a TOTALLY new concept all together. I've NEVER had that idea even cross my mind until right now. The idea of walking out of this mess with another person – they help me (really) and I help them (really) . . .

SILENCE	But I want to Scream
No words will ever adequately captivate RAD	I want RAD "captured" and quarantined and destroyed
WANT WORDS	THERE ARE NO WORDS (not enough . . . really)

And if you try to "fit" RAD
into words, I will be very
angry at you because you
just "minimized" RAD by
your "box of words"

IT WON'T FIT . . .
          EVER . . .
                    NEVER . . .
                              EVER . . .

Brainstorm ! ! No wonder . . . that's why
. . .

Sandy was right again. Journaling is such
an important and powerful technique in
the healing process of RAD and PTSD . . .

It gets the right hemisphere working

AND

It gets the left hemisphere working
too
TOGETHER . . .

So eventually you can problem-solve and get "out of the mess" of RAD.

That's probably what that EMDR stuff is attempting to do as well:

activate the right hemisphere . . .

which will then activate the left hemisphere . . .

which will eventually come to a solution or resolution for the whole of the brain and person . . .

At least for me, journaling has been THE key technique in helping me get as far as I have. To RAD people it has to be REAL (whatever the "it" is) . . . TANGIBLE . . . and journaling makes the "it" of ideas, data, feeling, information, etc. REAL and TANGIBLE – and CONTROLLABLE too . . .

I just thought that all of this sounds so VIOLENT . . . jungle war . . . Vietnam . . . "trauma" . . . brain damage . . .

Makes ME sound like a VIOLENT person . . . BUT I'M NOT ! !

The weird thing about this is that while it does FEEL violent and all . . .
    At the same time it doesn't . . . it feels surreal . . .

    IT FEELS NORMAL . . . and "normal" is just . . . well
    "Normal" and by definition NOT violent.

I can't describe it b/c as I look over what I've written . . . it reads like a horror movie . . . BUT IT'S NOT . . . well . . .

        it IS and at the same time it ISN'T . . .

        it's just "life" . . .

        it's just "whatever" . . .

        it's just "ok" . . .

* I'm beginning to think Sandy does get it. Why she's stuck with me I don't know – I wouldn't have stuck with me for this long that's for sure.

* It would be like watching a war movie with all the horror stuff going on . . . but the movie is in slow motion and there's "nice, mellow" music playing.

I'm NOT a MONSTER ! ! ! But when I read over what I've written . . . it makes me out to be one. NO . . . I'm a

> I was going to say "normal" person . . . but can't say "normal" . . . OK . . . I look and behave as normal as I can . . .

This is so frustrating . . .

OK . . . now add to the mix the RAD people who ARE really monsters – that come out in the form of narcissists, psychopaths, serial killers, anti-social, conduct disorder, borderline people.

I'm NOT one of them. I'm NOT like that. OK . . . some RAD people ARE that way I'm sure. And it's the RAD that's the "starter domino" behind all their violence and monster-ness.

THERE ARE NO WORDS . . .

I'm NOT a MONSTER. I'm NOT crazy or "mental" . . .

I'm . . . hurt . . . disorganized . . . confused . . . scared . . . learning delayed (life skills, I mean) . . . not of "this world" (the civilian world) . . . in culture shock . . . scared . . . brain hurt (I don't like the word "brain damaged" . . . but it's true) . . . in pain . . . numb . . . disconnected most of the time . . . and WANT OUT OF THIS JUNGLE . . .

I . . . try hard . . . I really do . . . I work hard . . . I try to do a good job at whatever I do . . . I try to get along with others (as best I can, I really do) . . . I pay my bills . . . I pay my taxes . . . I vote . . . I try . . . I really do try . . .

And I do want to be liked . . . and I do want somebody to love me . . . and I think I do at least look normal.

All this stuff is NOT me . . . it's INSIDE of me . . . Maybe that's the best way to try to describe it. It's INSIDE me . . . and I DON'T WANT IT TO BE THERE . . .

* I want to be loved . . . which means I need to let somebody close to me . . . but I can't let anybody close b/c it won't work out . . . they'll find out who I really am and leave . . . And I wouldn't blame them . . . but it's still too much of a risk.

I'm not a monster. I was a good dad - at least lots better than my Father was to me. I tried to be a good husband - and I was for the most part. My ex- will say I was over-controlling (and I can see that now) and would rage on occasion (which I can see now too). But all in all, I tried to be a good husband and father and think I succeeded for the most part.

AND . . . yet this stuff is INSIDE me. GET IT OUT ! ! ! !

And the reason I was over-controlling - to both of them - was that I didn't want anybody to GET HURT. And if everybody does things the way I have figured out . . . nobody will get hurt.

At least that was the thinking. I didn't want to be a "control freak" just to have the power and control. I didn't want anybody to GET HURT. I see now how that DID come across as unnecessary and over-controlling. I didn't see it then. I was just trying to survive and help them survive too. Even though they didn't NEED to "survive."

* But don't think for a moment that the journey is "over" and you're at "mission accomplished" . . . NOT YET . . . not even close . . . YET . . . (very random)

Once you do help me walk out of the jungle and get me to set my M16 and grenades down – WHICH I WILL BE VERY HESITANT TO DO THAT, by the way. I may just need to keep it for "security" reasons, "just in case," you know. – NOW YOU – since you're the one on this journey with me, you're now the "trauma medic" . . . NOW comes the PAINFUL part of opening up the wounds to clean them out . . . now comes the "thawing out" from all that numb – AND IT HURTS LIKE HECK ! ! Ask anybody who's suffered from frostbite what it felt like when their body parts began thawing out. Ask them . . . then multiply that X 100. And I

STILL won't really trust you . . . it's just the "lesser of 2 evils" now. And after all the blood stopping, suturing, medicating, bandaging, etc., etc., etc. . . . there's the "REHAB." This is where I need to re-define all those words and concepts I mentioned earlier.

* I can't wrap my brain around why Sandy is still willing to work with me. It can't just be the money . . . or at least it doesn't seem like it is to her.

* Realize physically is may take my body 2+ years – YES YEARS – to "re-regulate" to "normal" levels of stimuli or stress. You are helping me REHAB my:

> HEAD – thinking
> HEART – feelings
> BODY – connecting, cortisol levels, etc.

THAT SUCKS !!!

And "be HONEST with me Doc, how bad is it really?" Tell me straight and help me to rehab as far as I can –

100% rehab?
90%
65%
28% . . .
Whatever it is . . .

BE HONEST with me b/c I can read you very well and I'll know if you're lying to me. So help me and help yourself by shooting straight with me. I don't like the "beating around the bush" response stuff.

And once the bleeding has stopped, the bones have healed, the muscles can move again and the bandages are off . . . DON'T THINK FOR ONE MOMENT your job is "done" . . . NOT YET . . . BUT CLOSER . . .

* Realize as "stupid" as this may sound to you, I HAVE NO CLUE HOW TO BE A "CIVILIAN!!"

NO CLUE . . .

I don't know what civilians "do" . . .

say . . .

think about . . .

how/why they
laugh . . .

And I especially do NOT understand why
they DON'T carry an M16 with extra clips
around ALL THE TIME.

And why they don't wear their combat
boots, flak jacket and helmet ALL THE
TIME.

And why they don't double check to make
sure every "i" is dotted and every "t" is
crossed.

I don't know how civilians keep
themselves SAFE.

I'm not being melodramatic here . . . I
really do NOT get these things at all.

I don't know how/why civilians dream
and "plan for the future."

I REALLY HAVE NO CLUE ! ! !
AND IT'S NOT BECAUSE I'M
STUPID . . . IT'S BECAUSE I
NEVER HAD THE CHANCE TO

LEARN. I WAS BUSY LEARNING HOW TO SURVIVE . . . AND I MADE IT WHERE LESSER MEN DIDN'T.

I was learning "the ways" of a whole different world than you were. I don't know "the ways" of your world . . . the "civilian world" . . . what I dubbed "Normaltown, USA."

I mean, I spend all my time learning how to "Not Die" anyway I can . . . I don't know how to love, care, be tender –

> It's not that I WANT to HATE, HURT or BULLY people . . . NO . . .

> I DON'T KNOW HOW . . .

* I don't know how to empathize, "pick up on hints" and such –

> I NEVER LEARNED because I didn't (1) have the time and (2) didn't have a teacher and (3) didn't have a safe place to "learn" those civilian ways.

I don't know (really) how to CONNECT

- I THOUGHT I did, but now I see otherwise - to you . . .

> or myself . . .
> or my body for that matter.

I DON'T KNOW HOW. You will need to be my teacher and teach - and show - me all this "normal" stuff. You'll have to help me "re-calibrate" my body and emotions to a more accurate "normal" level and pace of life.

> - Which, by the way, will feel TOTALLY TOO SLOW, BORING and RIDICULOUS. I'm used to a "performance level" of survival as my normal pace of every day "living."

* I don't have anybody else close enough to me - yet - that can "reflect" back to me:
> (1) what's really normal
> (2) who I really am
> (3) what my real options are

I've spent all my life thinking I was
> STUPID . . .
> > SLOW . . .
> > > DENSE . . .

because I couldn't do or "get it" like other people could.

EVERYBODY else "gets it" . . .
EVERYBODY else just does it . . .
Why can't I?
  BECAUSE . . . I'M
     STUPID
     SLOW
     DENSE
     "SELFISH"
     LAZY
     "SELF FOCUSED"
     "IN MY OWN
       WORLD"
     UNCARING
     ALOOF

That's what I tell myself all the time . . . and believe it or not OTHER people tell / have told me those things too.

See . . . so it IS me. It IS all my fault. Which feeds into the control / survival thinking that I HAVE to be in control – even when I'm not – because I CANNOT BE HELPLESS. That's why it IS all my fault – because I have the control . . . I just wasn't quick enough . . . smart enough . . . to figure out the "right" answer in time – but I WILL find that "right" answer . . .

                        and thus the ROE
               gets added to
         again . . .

* NOW . . . FINALLY . . . AFTER HOW MANY YEARS
. . . I finally <u>DO</u> see that it —

     wasn't my fault . . .

          that I'm not STUPID
                    SLOW
                    DENSE
                    LAZY
                    UNCARING.

Always seem to be having the hanging words at
the end of a thought that don't fit on the page
where they belong. Stupid.

Yes, I DO see the "selfish" and the "self-focused"
. . . but that's because I HAD TO. That's what
survival does when you're all alone. I didn't
want to be that way, I just had to.

I DON'T KNOW

     BECAUSE

I WAS NEVER TAUGHT

     BECAUSE

THERE WASN'T A SAFE PLACE TO LEARN
"CIVILIAN" WAYS.

THAT'S WHY ! ! !

So, here I sit in this middle-aged body with the civilian "data base" of a neophyte (at BEST) . . .

It's embarrassing — but I've learned to hide any embarrassment very well. It's discouraging — but I've learned to trudge on come "hell or high water." It hurts when other's comment (usually in a "−" manner) about my social ineptness — but I'm learning to separate out the 2 different kinds of pain . . . This is the pain — I remind myself — that hurts (yes) but won't destroy me (no it won't) . . . but it still hurts.

It's confusing — and I know all too well how confusing can turn into chaos which turns into "RUN" survival mode all over again.

* I really think Sandy does. That's weird, after 4 years of therapy I'm just now seeing . . . or thinking . . . that she gets it and can help. And who's still in therapy after 4 YEARS !

Daha . . . a bit dense here aren't we?

* I don't want to be alone anymore. But I don't wish this on anyone either.

But I don't want to be alone . . . and not having anyone who "understands" reinforces the alone / isolation / walk alone yet again.

But it's really sad when the only person you can call a "friend" is your therapist!

Looking back over my other journal (not this one dedicated to my therapy homework stuff) I saw "I'm tired" over and over and over and over again. I also saw "I don't want to do this anymore" over and over and over again too . . .

"You can take the soldier out of the war . . . but . . ."

And when you do finally get the war "out" of the soldier . . .

It's still THERE to an extent . . . in the scars . . . the limp . . . the knuckle that freezes up.

Don't get me wrong . . . it is OVER . . . but the jungle war lasts until you take your last breath. I don't know if that's what real soldiers say it's like or not. But it's still THERE . . . in some way . . .

in some sense . . .
in some part of my body.

Please understand that part –

HEALING

Does NOT equal

"LIKE IT NEVER HAPPENED."

HEALING

DOES equal

"IT'S FINALLY OVER" . . . and now I can go on . . . in whatever shape I am . . . BUT YOU DON'T SEE

> the LIMP
> the SCARS
> the knuckle that freezes up . . .

so . . . you EXPECT me to move, think, act, feel, respond like I'm "normal" (like it never happened).

NO! – IT DID HAPPEN! AND EVEN THOUGH IT'S FINALLY OVER . . . IT ISN'T TOTALLY

That's why the lucky ones died. But you can't understand that. That's OK . . . it's not personal.

It's just the way it is and I know that
. . . and I'm OK with that – finally.

* I'm tired. There's still a lot of "point
tenderness" on my heart whenever I
think about – or talk about RAD. I think
I need go stop writing and thinking
about all of this. At least for a while. I
need to get grounded and
practice trying to "enjoy" life that I'm
realizing I do have now.

* My brain won't stop . . . I'm writing
again . . . never mind it's 3:25am.

* There's A LOT of things about this
civilian world I don't get. They place
so much attention on credentials, rank,
tenure, seniority, position, research, blah,
blah, blah . . . . . It even goes for all this
material on RAD I've been looking over.
The letters after a person's name, the
research methods, the this and the that
. . . I could have told them all of this
stuff – in time that is – and I don't have
ANY letters after my name or stripes on
my shoulder or a résumé full of
published works. Why? The only reason
I can think of is to keep the dumb,
stupid, lazy people out of a place of
power or influence so they can't do

damage to the society. That's just plain weird.

In my world – RAD – jungle war – the dumb, stupid, lazy people got picked off real quick like. Mortar shells don't home in on enlisted personnel only . . . grenades don't automatically roll away from Majors and toward Corporals . . . the "DIE" part of "DO or DIE" is the great equalizer . . . EXPERIENCE is the only QUALIFIER in my world . . .

> not letters following
>   your name
> not bars on your
>   shoulders
> not years
> not seniority pins.

EXPERIENCE = SURVIVING = STILL "STANDING" is the only "credentials" that really matter in the jungle. You don't have to worry about dealing with a dumb or stupid or lazy person for long – they'll get what they earned soon enough. It's not personal . . . that's just the way war / survival is . . . it IS survival of the fittest.

OK . . . OK . . . OK . . . I get it now.

131

THAT'S WHY RAD people have a hard time with authority. Because "rank" authority doesn't matter in the jungle . . .

Because unlike the REAL Vietnam where soldiers were fighting with their buddies and had other soldiers fighting alongside of them . . .

In the RAD jungle it's "Abandon ship. Every man for himself" and in that one phrase there IS NO RANK . . . there IS no SENIORITY . . . there IS NO AUTHORITY.

That makes sense now, why I HAVE to be IN CONTROL . . . because since it is "every man FOR HIMSELF" it really IS up to me and me alone.

It's NOT that I'm anti-authority . . . well maybe I am . . . It's that there just ISN'T ANY authority . . . as I see it . . . which conflicts with having a boss at work . . . Hummmmm . . . Something's sinking in here. Not sure what it is yet though.

Keep the body fit and trim to	Cover the body up with layers upon layers of fat to SHIELD or HIDE self
DEFEND self – or RUN	
(I can see this side of the polarization in both males and females)	(I can see this in females more, especially if they were sexually molested sometime in their childhood or adolescents.)

RAD impacts =

Right hemisphere of the brain
Left hemisphere of the brain
The amygdala part of the brain
Sleep patterns
Eating issues
Cognition
Relationships / social
        interactions
Physical body – over taxing the
        body
        auto immune system
        toxic adrenalin in the
            system Etc., etc., etc.,

Any spirituality a person has
Emotions / feelings
Learning abilities . . .

What does it NOT impact ? ? ? ?

NOTHING that comes to mind ! !

RAD impacts/encompasses 100% of the
person. NO part, place, segment of the
person is left
"UNDAMAGED" ! !

NONE . . .

And therapy wants to throw a "solution
focused" model at THAT?

I DON'T THINK SO . . .

Is there anything else that so totally
captivates a human being?

- sexual abuse comes to mind.
Especially if it's repeated . . .

Had to start on a fresh page.

So, now take a person who has RAD impacting 100% of their being . . .

+ (PLUS)

they were sexually abused (which probably impacts 100% of a person's being too) . . .

= (EQUALS)

A person so TOTALLY IMPACTED with PAIN, TRAUMA, TERROR, RAGE . . .

200% of the person had been DAMAGED ! !

So, "no rock goes unturned" in destroying and wrecking havoc on a person who experiences RAD + SEXUAL ABUSE ! !

Now do you at least begin to see why the lucky ones died? Even if you DO walk out of the jungle war finally . . . what do you have that wasn't fragged . . . cut . . . infected . . . cut with shrapnel, shot through ? ?

NOTHING is "intact" . . .

EVERYTHING is "shredded" –
skin, muscle, nerves, organs,
tendons, bone . . . all shredded.
My face wants to cry but there are no
tears. There never has been tears as long
as I can remember, but my face does this
"trying to cry" thing like it's doing now . . .

THAT'S what I look like when you finally
get a view – a good view – of me once
I'm out of the jungle. But you can't see
it . . . You think I'm over-reacting to get
attention or something or . . .

LOOK AT IT AGAIN. What part of a
human life DIDN'T GET TOTALLY
DAMAGED by RAD + SEXUAL ABUSE ? ?

You tell me? Am I just "spinning a
story" here or am I . . . maybe . . . just
maybe . . . telling the truth here?

And maybe it's a truth you can't
comprehend.

That doesn't make it not the truth.

You do the work – write down all the
areas of a human life/existence that are
impacted by sexual abuse =

write it all down
list it all

make sure your "research is
complete"

NOW . . . what's left off the
collective list?

What part of me – or any human
being surviving this –
is "untouched" or "uninjured" or
"unhurt"???

> Name it if you can because
> I CAN'T.

And it really is true – "But for the grace
of God." I can't explain it any other
way. Not really . . . not as someone who
experientially knows and understands . . .

> But . . .

> "For the grace of God!"

So why is there NO "TIME" in the jungle
war? Simple – it's NOW or NEVER (the
polarization thing again).

See if this makes any sense:

NOW   **NEVER**

Avoid "Loss" by   Causes LOSS
Doing, eating, etc.
NOW

Run from PAIN   Causes PAIN

Don't get "destroyed"   PAIN = me"

                MO "Don't Die"

NOTHING is "SECURE" so . . .

> Eat – NOW
> Decide – NOW
> Hide – NOW
> "Enjoy" it – NOW
> Grab it – NOW ! ! !

There is no "TIME" to "see what's happening" . . .

> Exactly like she said, there is no OBJECT PERMANENCE . . . so there is no "it'll be here tomorrow."

> Because . . . in a jungle war . . . there is NO "tomorrow."

> I could be DEAD by then . . .

> "Surviving" is ALWAYS in the "NOW!"

"NO TIME" adds a stress level/pressure all its own . . . which only adds to all the OTHER stress/pressure and trauma inside.

An environment of abuse, chaos, trauma, neglect, abandonment, fear, etc. CREATES RAD . . .

- the RAD itself then CREATES a heck of an environment all its own (internally and sometimes externally too) . . .

EXTERNAL WORLD = AWFUL

INTERNAL WORLD = AWFUL

THERE IS NO "SAFE" PLACE WHAT-SO-EVER . . . ANYWHERE . . . ANYTIME . . . EVER

And when both the external and internal worlds feel like heck

DAHA !

of course there's gonna be no "self-regulation!"

I could have told anybody THAT without having any letters after my name. How could you "regulate" in that place?

> Nothing external to help
> regulate you
> Nothing internally to help you
> regulate

* no "compass bearing" in either world so the compass is of no use/worth/value . . .

> NOW =
> > Hoard it
> > Grab it
> > Do it
> > Take it
> > Don't do it
> > Use it
> > "Experience" it
> > Get it
> > Steal it
> > Touch, taste it
> > Answer it
> > Get it "over with"

Because the ONLY thing that IS "SECURE" / SURE . . . is the PAST

> AND

> > it's not in the "PAST" until it's "OVER WITH"

NOW . . .

* That's why there's so much lack of impulse control with us RAD people. ESPECIALLY when we're children or teens.

NO SAFE

+

NO OBJECT PERMANENCE (really)

=

"NOW" = NO IMPULSE CONTROL and no REASON for exercising any impulse control either.

Is that so hard to understand? If I was adopted from an orphanage (anywhere) or was caught in the foster care system and you bring me home to what you see as a "safe" environment. Do you really think all this is just going to "go away" if you just "love" me enough ? ? ?

* If my childhood was a more-chaotic-environment-than-you realized when you married me . . . and you're not clued in to this whole world of the jungle war – the RAD – do you think just getting away from my family will "fix" this problem ? ?

Do you think if you just love me enough . . . or take me to church enough . . . or give me enough discipline and structure – regardless of my age – that this will solve my problems ? ?

* Looking back I am sorry for the crazy-ness I put my Mother and Father through.

I'm sorry for all the crazy-ness and rage my ex- lived through.

I'm truly sorry for all the mess and crazy-ness I put my son through.

I didn't mean it. But that's not an excuse either.

It didn't start out as my fault . . . but became my fault when I did what I did to them.

* Trying to keep this objective has gone into the trash. That's OK . . . it's just for me. Wouldn't want to put anybody through the craziness of trying to make any sense of this. Anyway . . .

(Next page)

The amygdala part of the brain only understands NOW

... if the right hemisphere isn't "open" and working

and if the left hemisphere isn't "open" and working – the sequential side that does understand time: past – present – future ...

the only thing the brain DOES KNOW – UNDERSTANDS – GRASPS – is NOW !

What else could the brain think ? ! ? ! ?

* See how "Never make a mistake" ROE tactic fits in? Since the NOW is all that exists . . .

and if I do make a mistake NOW . . .

it's a mistake – FOREVER . . .

and it can't be "fixed" in the future . . . b/c there IS no "later" to "fix" it because there is no TIME . . . and besides . . . this may be the one decision /

mistake that could cost me my
life –

it only takes 1 mistake / 1
error / 1 stupid thing to get
yourself killed up in the jungle

JUST ONE . . . THAT'S ALL IT
    TAKES = ONE . . . "1."

People who make mistakes don't
survive long in the jungle war. And it
only takes ONE . . . little . . . simple . . .
"harmless" mistake . . . and it's over . . .

1 stupid step
1 thoughtless moment
1 didn't double-check your clip
1 dozing off soundly
just 1 . . .

For the want of a nail the shoe was
lost.
For the want of the shoe the horse was
lost.
For the want of the shoes the rider
was lost.
For the want of the rider the battle was
lost.
For the want of the battle the

kingdom was lost.
And all for the want of a horseshoe
nail[9].

It's some poem or proverb I remember
my Father made me memorize as a child.
Interesting I can still remember it word
perfect after all these years? ALL
BECAUSE OF ONE STUPID "NAIL!"

There is no "mercy" or "grace" in jungle
wars. Yes, I may "get lucky" and NOT
killed b/c of this 1 dumb thing I did . . .
but I WON'T be lucky ever again . . . you
can BET on that . . .

That's why a RAD person ALWAYS has to
be RIGHT – even if they really aren't...
they have to skew reality to still keep
the perception of "right" so to NOT have
made a stupid mistake so to "NOT DIE."

> So . . . I try VERY HARD to do
> everything "RIGHT" – PERFECTLY–
> and if / when I don't . . . I have
> to rationalize it until that was the
> "RIGHT" thing anyway.

> Being "WRONG" = getting hurt = DIE.

> I don't want to DIE . . .

So I will NEVER be "WRONG" . . .

EVER . . . EVER . . .

NOPE . . . I WILL
NOT BE WRONG !

And if I DO come face to face with being / doing something "wrong" (remember EVERYTHIG is black or white) I have to "fix" it RIGHT NOW . . .

Because it's too late, it HAS to be "FIXED" NOW !

Even if I don't know HOW to fix it . . . I have to do SOMETHING to fix it NOW!

As disorganized and chaotic as RAD is . . .

as random as the listing in the ROE may be . . .

there is ONE CENTER POINT . . . one logical purpose . . . one thing

everything else is organized around = the MO "DON'T DIE."

THAT is CLEAR.

THAT is "ORGANIZED"

THAT is "LOGICAL" . . .

There is no "mushy" . . .
"un-certainty" . . . about
THIS ONE THING.

EVERYTHING is
"ORGANIZED" around this goal.

Polarization (again):

Dis-organized (in general)	Overly organized (around the MO)
Easily distracted	1 Central focus

* So, how does a person help the RAD person? How have I "helped" myself? I'm not sure. I just DID all this. I started reading, and journaling on RAD. I don't know how to tell another person "Here's where you'll find your child, friend in the jungle."

I can't do that.

They – like me – don't even know where they are (where I was).

* Wait, somebody mentioned something about Reactive Attachment Disorder in the context of issues they were having with their adopted daughter. I don't remember . . . Oh yea . . . they were in the booth next to me at the restaurant last week – it seems like a lifetime ago now. That phrase stuck, RAD, and so I did an internet search on it and all this began to unravel piece by piece, article by article, book by book . . .

So what's the answer to it? I can't give an answer because there are too many variables in the jungle:

    where they are
    where the mountains are
    how high the river is
    where it's muddy
    where's the danger
    variable after variable after
    variable . . .

    and the jungle is always
    changing too

Yes, once you do get me out of the jungle and begin doing trauma surgery some things will become protocol

addressing the depression

dealing with any eating issues – or official disorders

dealing with anxiety

dealing with the likelihood of perfectionism

dealing with any sleep problems that are here

grieving the losses – of things actually "lost" and things "never had in the first place"

connecting mind, heart and body together

coming out of PTSD

finding purpose & meaning in life

finding who I really was meant to be

* Yes, there may be techniques and ways to work/help me with each of these areas. BUT what do you do first? I can't prescribe a pre-prescribed how to triage for every person. Every person will triage differently. It HAS to be that way.

But I DO know this . . . you have to deal with the RAD issues FIRST before you can really get anywhere with the other important issues.

And it's all connected. The sleep problems will impact my concentration and ability to deal with the RAD stuff. The depression will also diminish my ability to think and deal with the RAD stuff. The anxiety issues – especially if it's to the level of OCD patterns will interrupt my working on the RAD stuff.

BUT . . . however you do it . . . THE RAD STUFF MUST BE ADDRESSED FIRST AND FOREMOST.

* When you have a dual-diagnosis (co-occurring disorder) person (chemical addiction + depression) triage says you deal with the addiction FIRST. Because if you don't the addiction will always confound any work you attempt to do with the depression. Yes, they are "chicken and egg" connected. But you have to address the chemical addiction first.

So too with RAD. You have to deal with the RAD first.
UNLESS . . . If you have RAD + other stuff + a chemical addiction . . .

THEN you deal with:

(1) chemical addiction (whatever it may be)
(2) RAD
(3) all the other things in whatever order they need to be dealt with.

* If you took the time, had the heart, and honed your jungle skills enough to even FIND me – whether I'll admit it to you or not – you've at least earned some of my respect. Maybe not my trust . . . but at least some of my respect . . . and that's something NOBODY else has done to this point in my life. You have to know the ways of this jungle. You have to know the reasons and "logic" written in the ROE. And while you need to keep your own healthy boundaries, you can't flinch when I aim my M16 at you and squeeze the trigger – which I will do . . . because in the FRIEND or FOE polarization world of the jungle warfare . . .

I haven't found any FRIEND yet ...
everyone is seen as FOE . . . that's
because everyone CAN hurt me —
they have the POTENTIAL to hurt me
. . . so they're automatically a FOE
. . . and so are you . . . at least in
the BEGINNING.

* I can't count the times people have
tried to reach out to me to "help." They
tried for a time and all of them finally
gave up and stopped calling, talking with
me, inviting me out for dinner. I mean,
I don't BLAME them for walking away
. . . I would walk away from myself if
I could. So it's not their fault . . . but it
didn't help either. In fact, the
walking away only reinforced the rules
in the ROE to "never let anyone close
because they WILL walk away from you
sooner or later."

And this part doesn't fit into words
either. Yes, it's centered in the
relationship between them and me.
Yes, there are the social boundaries
that need to be maintained but the
how . . .
    when . . . why . . . where . . . has to
    be felt — lived out — experientially
    walking with me. And it will take

YEARS . . . believe me.

AND . . .

that's not even addressing the added boundary issues you need to take when you add in PTSD and/or sexual abuse.

Yes, I remember re-defining things like:

Safe
Trust
Pain
"Normal"
"OK"
and all those things.

* I remember working time after time to get the PTSD flashbacks and nightmares to be over.

I remember listing (I think I had over 6 pages by the time it was done) all the losses in my life.

Yes, I remember the "grounding techniques" Sandy taught me – and had to practice over and over and over again.

I remember writing out as many of the

rules in the ROE as I could – and tried to look at them from an "adult-today" perspective to see what was viable and what wasn't for the civilian world.

I remember looking for "modern tactics" I could use to keep myself safe – now – in Normaltown, USA.
Yes, I journaled and journaled and journaled.

> I'm using the word "journaling" . . . I just realized that! And that's probably why Sandy has been smiling lately when we talk about my "journaling." It's not just "writing" anymore.

> Huummmmmmmmmmmmmmmmmmmm . . .

Wonder when it changed? Have to go back and look sometime.

* I remember that I talked with a few people about these things. My ex- knows most of this stuff now. Strange how we seem to get along just fine as long as I'm not a key part of her life. And I don't blame her, but it's good to have somebody to at least talk to.

Yes, I've wrestled and wrestled and fought with the "Why, God?" questions and confusion. Yes, I fought. Yes, I wrestled. And bit-by-bit I surrendered to God and to His sovereignty. How? By fighting with Him, by wrestling with Him, by asking "Why?" many, many times.

And yes, I remember the risk after risk I took – each one as scary as the one before – to consciously choose to do something differently, or to think differently.

* I remember finally letting myself want another motorcycle – it was terrifying! And then I got another motorcycle – and I was terrified that it'd get taken away or wrecked somehow (the loss thing again). And I remember wanting a different one then the one I just got – THAT was even more terrifying because it meant I wasn't "satisfied with what I had" so God would find a way to take it away from me because I wasn't "thankful" enough for what I had. All the TERROR because if a MOTORCYCLE! A "thing." How crazy is that? But the ALL or NOTHING and all the other ROEs apply to motorcycles the same way they do to anything. I remember how hard

it was to WANT . . . to let myself really WANT something . . . To HOPE for something . . . That TOO is risky business.

And that was followed by "What do I really want anyway?" I DON'T KNOW...I really don't . . . There's no time in the jungle war to contemplate what you "want" or "like" or "prefer" in life.

And the motorcycle carrousel of buy, sell, buy again . . . shows that I really didn't know what I wanted - even when it comes to something fairly simple as "What motorcycle do I want?"

* That's part of learning how to be a civilian - learning the "What do I want?" and the "What do I really like/don't like?" That goes for EVERYTHING from motorcycles, to vacations, to work environments, to friends, to clothes . . . EVERYTHING. I never bought shoes based upon what I "liked" or "wanted." Shoes "had" to be bought based upon:

> (1) need
> (2) practicality - do they "work" well

(3) the absolutely best shoe for the money

because it' ALL or NOTHING . . . RIGHT or WRONG . . .

All of this over a pair of SHOES ! !

It never occurred to me to think what I'd "like" – even in COLOR – Color was chose on practicality PERIOD. End of discussion.

It was hard to let myself even begin to "want" or "like." I do remember giving myself OFFICIAL PERMISSION to be allowed to "want" and "like" NOW.

"It's OK . . .
NOW."

* I remember STILL desiring to be SAFE and took a risk to look over all the ROE to see if they "really" helped me be safe or not OR . . . maybe they did BACK THEN . . . but don't – or do at too big of a cost NOW . . . It's like fighting with play bows and arrows because that's all I had as a 5 year old.

But . . . as an adult / NOW . . . I can learn to use "grown up" and "civilian" tactics to keep myself safe. Things like:

I have a voice now. I can and will be heard.

I can negotiate and cooperate with people.

And . . . if necessary . . . I still have my M16 not too far out of reach. But I don't have to have it cocked and locked slung at my ready.

* Notice how much of my thinking revolved around military/warfare metaphors and word pictures? I was never in the military. I was the "military brat" but not in it myself. I'm not doing that on purpose it just seems to make the most sense to my brain –
the closest OUTSIDE reality that describes my INSIDE world . . .

And I've never been the actual sailor on

the OUTSIDE so maybe I'm out to lunch. But that's the only thing I can imagine to use to try and show what's going on inside.

* I was hoping in all this journaling that I might be able to figure out at least a general path to helping RAD people.

I KNOW there's help – I know there's a way out – I KNOW it can be over. I made it out of the RAD jungle. I've talked with a couple of others (even though they didn't call it this) who have made it out too. So I KNOW it can be done . . .

> What CAN'T be done is to tell another person exactly "how to" . . . it doesn't matter whether that "other person" is a friend, spouse, child, patient or whatever.

That's it . . .

> IT CANNOT BE "TOLD"

> IT CAN ONLY BE LIVED OUT (2 PEOPLE) TOGETHER . . .

That's the only way . . . Really . . . and I don't know if that can fit into a 45 minute 1 time per week "therapeutic relationship" – maybe – I guess it's been done but I don't know for sure. But it usually included more than just a therapist 1 X per week.

BUT . . . that's what Sandy's been doing. She just gives me lots of homework to research, write, read, etc.

And the other person doesn't have to be a RAD person

Sandy isn't.

It can be a person that at least "gets it" as much as a non-RAD person can. So it could be a spouse, parent, friend, mentor, or somebody like that. But it won't be an easy road and it won't be a quick fix – even if you pray about it.

* Once they got to the "readjustment to civilian life" phase . . . there's STILL no "how to" exactly. Again, it's living with them. That phase does feel a bit like parenting then – yes, you teach things formally and yes, you teach on what comes up when it comes up. Again, you

WALK THROUGH LIFE with the person explaining and teaching along the way . . . until they're ready to "launch" out of the "nest" (that they never had left before) . . . and if it's a therapist-client relationship – by that time the person (patient) feels more like "family" than "client" – even if you keep healthy therapist- client boundaries.

Yes, the professional boundaries need to be kept – but . . . I don't know how to put it into words.

I guess if it ever happens that I can help another RAD person (not as their therapist but as just "another person") it would be like an orphan finding another orphan . . .

"We were soldiers once . . ."

"We were orphans once . . ."

We know . . . we understand . . . we have a common "blood" . . .

* Random thought. I remember watching a TV documentary a long time ago about a WWII Japanese soldier on one of the Philippine Islands who was still "fighting"

the war 20 or so years AFTER it was officially over. He was still following his ROE (his orders) and his orders did NOT include paper flyers falling out of the sky or megaphones hung from aircraft saying the war was over. He finally came out (if I remember the story right) only AFTER a superior officer he recognized came in and had him "stand down." He followed his ROE - his orders - his code, like a good soldier is supposed to do. I understand that. I laughed when they tried the flyer and megaphone things. I could have told you those tactics would not have worked.

YOU HAVE TO ENTER INTO THE WAR TO PULL THE SOLDIER OUT.

Anyway, maybe living in Manila for a while made the story more intriguing to me. But the story has stuck in my mind because I can relate . . . somehow . . . as crazy as that may sound . . . there's something in that story that I can recognize in myself.

* I'm STILL wrestling with "what takes the place of the old MO ('Don't Die')?" The old MO was what "motivated" all of me:

To keep going
To get up in the morning
To go to work
To "do" just about EVERYTHING
I do.

There was NO CHOICE before . . . I just "did" it . . . I just kept going . . .

BUT NOW? . . . As that MO goes away . . .

WHAT IS THERE TO
MOTIVATE ME NOW?

WHY get up in the morning?
WHY work?
WHY . . . ?
WHY . . . ?
What's the rest of the sentence: "I get
up BECAUSE _____?"

I DON'T KNOW ! !

---

* I feel like an idiot.

* Along with the MO change thing has been the HUGE desire NOT TO EXIST either. The MO is fading but the "NOT

EXIST" is STILL here ! What do I to with THAT?

WHY "exist" anyway?
WHY . . . ? ?

What's the rest of this sentence: "I EXIST BECAUSE _____?"

All these changes and risks bring a real sense of physical pain/distress along with them.

Not only do I feel the aches and pains a body has (that I was numb to all these years) – but all these other things bring a sense of physical pain as well (or @ least "discomfort" which gets interpreted as "pain") with them. "Growing Pains." Really PAIN.

AND . . . I do NOT know HOW to manage/deal with pain. I NEVER LEARNED how to – I just dissociated/numbed out. That all I learned what to do with pain.

So what do I do NOW? I feel trapped . . .

I feel WORSE, not "BETTER" . . .

I want to go back to the "old"
way of not feeling

B/C I DON'T KNOW HOW TO
MANAGE PAIN AS A CIVILIAN.

* I NEVER got to learn . . . and besides
. . . since numb/dissociation worked so
well I did it over and over and over
again – because it DOES WORK . . .

the more it works . . .

the more I use it . . .

the more I use it . . .

the better it works . . .

etc., etc., etc.
(and I didn't have the time to learn any
other way)

THAT'S NOT FAIR !

Moving from:

NUMB   FEELING
FROSTBITE   THAWING OUT

The 1st and HUGE thing you experience is PAIN ! ! And lots of it. And you don't have any skills to handle it . . . so you . . . survive . . . through it . . . you WANT IT OUT . . . you ENDURE . . . just like I did in the jungle war all those years before. SO WHAT'S "BETTER" about this feeling thing? What's so good about "normal?"

> "Normal" (civilian living) doesn't feel very good AT ALL !

> I want to go back to "Egypt" – the old way – the jungle war way . . .

Not because it's any better . . . but BE-CAUSE I DON'T WANT TO HURT ANY MORE . . .

> Can't other people understand at least THAT part of RAD?

* "Life sucks . . . then you die" – but not soon enough !

That's why I believe the lucky ones died.

* All of this is going on INTERNALLY with me while EXTERNALLY I'm trying – STILL – to "not stand out" at work and at church. I'm trying to look/be as

"normal" as possible. And since other people don't see the scars, limp and frozen knuckles . . . they LOOK at me as "normal" and EXPECT "normal" out of me – NORMAL ADULT that is . . . not a jungle war SURVIVED CHILD like it feels inside.

* Now that I finally stopped running from the phantom freight train that was about to run me over . . .

Yes, the "stopping" feels good – a relief – finally

But what do I do NOW?

HOW do I "rest?"

WHY go on?
"Go on" to WHERE?

At what PACE do I "go on" at?

What's the PURPOSE? Is there any purpose to "go on"?

I DON'T KNOW . . .

I DON'T KNOW . . .

I REALLY DON'T.

After how many years of this journey and I STILL have to consciously tell my muscles and jaw to RELAX . . . over and over and over and over again . . . – 3 x since writing this one sentence !

UGGGGGGGH ! ! !

More polarizations:

| Don't want to BEAR this HURT any more | Can't let anybody else BEAR this HURT for me |

That's one more of the ROE

> "Can't let anybody else get hurt because of me."

Why? =

(1) EVIL HURT me
(2) EVIL = HURT
(3) HURT = EVIL
(4) Therefore, If I HURT someone
    – or if they get HURT because of me (or by my existence in any way) = I'm EVIL
(5) I don't want to be EVIL so . . .
(6) I HAVE to MAKE SURE (guarantee) no one, under any circumstance,

for any reason ever gets HURT because of me, or else that . . .

(7) that makes ME EVIL too!

That's why Jesus dying "in my place" is soooooooooooo hard for me. I'm NOT worthy of that. I'm not WORTHY at all PERIOD. In fact "WORTH" doesn't even EXIST with me.

Why?

(1) because bad things DON'T happen to good people

(2) bad things DID happen to me

(3) therefore I'm NOT a "good person" which means, I'm a BAD person

(4) because bad things DO happen to bad people - b/c they deserve it.

* So the self-contempt/self-anger is legitimate! It makes sense to hate what's detestable/unworthy.

Besides . . . to HURT somebody else with all this RAGE would make me EVIL . . . I can take it out on me and still not be EVIL then.

It all has a "logic" to it. It all fits into the ROE.

* More polarizations

There must be a small part of me that still wants to love.

I firmly believe I'm un-lovable and not even worth attempting to be loved

I don't want to be ALONE anymore

I can't let anybody close enough to NOT be LONELY

UGGGGH-again . . .

And besides, I wouldn't want any of this to "spill" over onto another person — they don't deserve that.

* Think about it. What would it be like to live 24/7 with a person who totally hates you . . .

Thinks you're worthless and believes it's all your fault?

How "fun"/"enjoyable" would living like that be? THAT'S what RAD is like. I live with myself and that's how I see myself - and treat myself ! !

And why would I want to impose that onto anybody else? Nobody deserves to have to live with me in this state. Nobody. Yes, my parents were jerks, but they didn't deserve how I treated them. My ex- didn't deserve being married to me and my son didn't deserve having to be trapped under all this stuff. I didn't see it then. I thought it was all their faults - then. Now, I see most of it (not all) it was really my fault.

* Learning to do PMR (Progressive Muscle Relaxation) helped, I think, for several reasons:

> (1) to learn how to relax - in a very concrete way
> (2) to learn to detect tension in my body
> (3) to connect mind and body
> (4) to slow down the racing in my brain

I still use it. I still NEED to use it.

* More polarizations:

| Want somebody to come and RESCUE me | Won't let anybody close enough to accept HELP from anyone. |

* When you talk about "surrendering to God," that takes on a whole different meaning to a RAD person – and likely more biblically ACCURATE – then most Western Christians see . . .

SURRENDER is a MILITARY term that comes at THE END . . .

> When all other resources and options have failed
> When there is no other course. It is NOT "negotiating."
>
> The image that sticks in my mind is of a Japanese General handing his Samurai sword over to an American General on a naval warship. That sword represents (because it actually is) the last, final and closest weapon he can use to keep himself SAFE. NOW – his life – or death – is in the hands of

another = his former enemy.

There can NEVER be true surrender without a FIGHT first – "to the end" kind of FIGHT. The USA does NOT know surrender – except for the Confederate States during the Civil War . . .

Follow the sequence / logic of RAD:

ALL CONTROL or NO control
(polarized thinking)

NO control = DIE

SURRENDER = NO control

SURRENDER = DIE . . . and the MO shouts   "DON'T
DIE!"

* So "go down fighting" if you must but you do NOT die . . . ever . . .

It's not an "honor" thing = "Death before dishonor" mantra. It's the MO under the ROE . . . under everything RAD knows and feels and believes . . .

* So how did I get to the point where I DID finally surrender to God? I know it was a HUGE FIGHT. I know it was DESPERATE. I know it was TERRIFING. I know I felt as though I WAS going to physically DIE . . .

> but it came to a point where there WAS NO OTHER OPTION.

> There it is . . . It WAS:
>   (1) Keep FIGHTING (and
>   die for sure)

>   OR

>   (2) SURRENDER (and maybe
>   die . . . but maybe not
>   die). It was the "lesser
>   of 2 PAINS."

In a sense . . . SURRENDER was following the MO . . . "traumatic bonding" to God – in a good sense that is . . . "As a POW, maybe I can STILL _____ and get away or at least 'not die'."

SURRENDERING is NOT the same as TRUSTING – NOT at all. But as the surrender occurred it opened up the opportunity for me to SEE GOD AS HE

REALLY IS . . . and that opened up the way to realize He truly is TRUSTWORTHY . . . maybe . . . and maybe a little bit more . . . and maybe . . . I'm not sure, but that's how it seems to have come about. I do remember sooooooo many things changing / crashing / falling apart all at the same time when the surrendering process happened –

Definitions were changing
Feelings were emerging
Perceptions were being challenged
    and altered
Memories were coming back
The body was feeling "different"
Feeling DESPERATE – I remember
    feeling that a lot
Feeling TERROR
Facing 1 risk after another after
    another – EACH as hard as the
    one before, if not more so.

Sandy being here through it all.

* I don't know – I can't tell yet – if there was an actual sequence to all of this. It was like having multiple surgical procedures being done on different parts of my being – all SEPARATE but all CONNECTED somehow –

even thought they may not have seemed connected at the time. It was a complicated process with lots of "do-overs" along the way.

The picture that comes to mind is that of putting the legs and braces of a wooden chair together. You cannot do just 1 piece at a time. You must do all 4 legs plus the braces that inter-connect the legs together all at the same time. That's part of the strength of the chair. The CORPORATE strength. They are inter-connected. I learned that lesson the hard way - by trying to methodically do one piece at a time on that antique chair I got that time. It won't work . . . so I learned. That's a little piece of how the "multiple surgical procedures" may be like.

I don't think the "healing" can be done SOLO. I really don't think a person can. I'm a diehard SOLO type of person - and like "going solo" too. But THIS journey? NO . . . you can only gain a sense of yourself because of being in relation with other people.

NO PEOPLE = NO SELF CONCEPT = NO SELF

And I don't know what to call it but there MUST be a deep kind of connection - KINDRED SPIRIT

SOUL MATE

? _____ ?

Even if it's kept within healthy boundaries of the patient-therapist ethics like Sandy has been able to do. There still HAS to - I believe - be that "SOMETHING MORE" than ONLY the "genuine empathy" and "unconditional positive regard" of a professional therapist.

Anyway . . .

* The person has to be a "leader" . . . but NOT the generic leader type our culture talks so much about. Like my definition of a leader:

> (1) Can't be afraid to die - If you're going to lead me into "hell and back" . . . and you're afraid to die . . . you won't lead "into hell" . . . you'll just send me - and I can't trust that.

(2) Can't be afraid to live – If you're going to lead me into "hell and back" . . . and you're afraid of living . . . you won't fight hard enough to bring me "back" – and I can't trust that either.

(3) Head grounded in REALITY – NOT "head in the sand" . . . not "head in the clouds" . . . grounded in reality. That's the world I know. And I need you to talk straight and true to me – otherwise I can't trust you. What REALLY are our chances of getting out alive? Tell me the truth.

(4) Make solid / realistic decisions. You "lead" by decisions – if you can't decide – I can't trust you to know what you're doing / or where you're going. If your decisions aren't solid and realistic – I can't trust you.

(5) Go first. I FOLLOW . . . behind the leader. You have to – not "just be willing to" go first. GO FIRST. In some REAL way, you have to have GONE FIRST – so that you "know" – and I can trust that.

In the corporate and Christian world we go through "leaders" and managers and CEOs left and right. In any war zone it's DO or DIE

GOOD LEADERS = DO

BAD LEADERS = DIE . . . or get their troops KILLED . . . or both

It's THAT simple. And even with a good leader there are NO GUARANTEES. Remember . . . WAR sifts out the dumb, stupid and lazy very quickly . . . by KILLING THEM . . .

and the men under their command.

Ask a Hanoi Hilton POW survivor about "surrender" and the "life" of a "surrendered person." Ask them what's at stake when you surrender. Ask them about any "guarantees" the surrendered POW really has. That's what RAD feels like / thinks like / lives like.

It HAS to be MY FAULT. Follow the RAD logic here:

If it's MY FAULT . . . then I can fix it somehow

Which means I have the CONTROL somehow . . .

I just didn't find the CONTROL soon enough . . . this time . . . but I'll keep looking because it IS there . . . somewhere . . .

I DO HAVE THE CONTROL

* When I begin to entertain the idea that it may NOT be my fault that means I may NOT be able to "fix" it

If I can't fix it no matter WHAT I do . . . that means I am POWERLESS

If I'm POWERLESS then I can't follow – ENSURE – my MO "Don't Die."

So you see, it HAS to be MY FAULT . . . it HAS to.

So when you talk to me and tell me it wasn't my fault it's hard to believe. There's so much more tied into MY FAULT than whose fault it really was. You may see it as a simple my fault vs. his – her fault thinking change (perception shift) but to me . . . it's LIFE or DEATH

DO   or   DIE
CONTROL   or   NO CONTROL
ALL   or   NOTHING

* Remember, I don't deal in concepts very well. I only live/react in REALITY - NOW. Words don't count because they're not REAL. Only what is REAL can be "BELIEVED" =

"My fault"
"Your fault"
"Their fault" . . . what difference does it really make? Does it change what happened? No. Does it change the pain? No. Will it "fix" things for the future for me? No. SO WHAT USE IS IT? I don't get it.

* Can you begin to understand the thinking process of RAD? We DON'T think like you do. We don't. If your thinking is like a color photograph . . . my thinking is like the color negative - everything is flipped/opposite. And with a B&W print (since I think in polarized black or white anyway) what's "white" to you is what to me?

Black.

What's normally black to
you is what to me?

White.

* OK, this dates me. With everything
gone to digital photography now nobody
will understand the color negative thing.
Oh well . . . doesn't matter anyway . . .

Even the GRAY shades are reversed and
opposite.

* "The lucky ones died."

"But for the grace of God . . . "

BOTH statements are true for RAD people.
At least some of us.

* RAD breeds RAD . . . breeds RAD . . .
breeds RAD.

OF COURSE IT DOES ! ! !

Now THAT was random!

* It's very hard to have real relationship
with a RAD person b/c . . . they either see

you as a FOE . . .

OR . . .

see you as COMPETITION for "limited" resources – which makes you a FOE.

I see a lot of borderline personality disorder traits in RAD:

Black vs. white polarized thinking
"Go away – don't leave me"
All or nothing
Creating chaos (because it's familiar)
Creating the triangle "drama"
(1) there's a HERO ("friend")
(2) there's a VILLAIN ("foe")
(3) there's a VICTIM –
borderline person will always script themselves in the victim role.

And the other person (not the borderline person) will get scripted back and forth – often changed without any warning – between being the HERO ("come close") and the VILLAIN ("go away").

* Maybe RAD is a key ingredient behind many of the Axis II personality disorders. Would seem to make sense to me. It would be an important element behind the disorders. Don't know if any research has been done on that or not. Oh well . . . just a thought.
* Part of the re-defining of TERMS needs to include:

> Fair
> Unfair
> "My fault"
> Responsible
> Mistake
> Wrong

* OK some ideas after learning stuff on crisis/stress[10].

(oops, not enough space. Next page)

(1) Living "stress free" would look like this:

DEMANDS  RESOURCES

(equal)

There's a balance between
Resources and Demands.
Every "demand" can be attended
to by a "resource" that's
already accessible

"RAD living" looks/feels like this:

DEMANDS

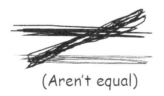

(Aren't equal)

RESOURCES

In a survival mode, ALL situations and ALL "demands" seem HUGE and overwhelming . . . or . . . potentially overwhelming = DIE

Resources – in a survival situation ALWAYS seem to be scarce. Besides the only "skill" I've learned is how to "Not Die". So my "resources" ARE in fact minimal

And in proportion to my real "limited" resources . . . almost any demand is seen as HUGE.

(2) The "Reactions to Trauma"

(A) Physical –

Tremors/tics, etc.
GI issues/nausea
Fatigue
Headaches
Sleep problems
> Don't know about raised BP levels

(B) Cognitive –

Confusion (often/some)
Poor cause & effect problem-
solving
Distractibility
In-attention
Hyper-vigilant
Heightened alertness

(C) Behavioral –

Sleep problems
Nightmares
Appetite disturbance – "food
issues"
Hyper-vigilant (again)
Startle response (related to
heightened alertness)
Withdrawal from crowds
Isolation

(D) Emotional –

Guilt
Anger
Fear
Anxiety
SHOCK
Sadness
Hopelessness

Irritability
NUMBNESS

MOST, IF NOT ALL, OF THESE THINGS ARE "NORMAL" LIVING CONDITIONS FOR A LOT OF RAD PEOPLE . . .

* Stress/TRAUMA events are etched into the brain with a HIGH emotional "CHARGE" connected to them – deeply etched.

NON-traumatic events do NOT have a huge emotional "charge" connected to them so may not even get RECORDED at all in the memory of a person experiencing trauma often.

Therefore reinforcing the notion that ALL of life is UNSAFE . . .

> Because only the UNSAFE (traumatic) got recorded into the memory.

Weird . . . but that would make sense.

* OK . . . OK . . . OK . . . another "bit" I remember from my childhood is that I

was always being told "now, don't forget
. . ." whatever it was. If I really was
always forgetting . . . maybe it's because
of the numbness or things just not
getting recorded into my memory bank
in the first place. Hummmmm. But that
would make sense because I don't ever
remembering trying to forget things
because the forgetting often came back
to bite me somehow. I don't know. But it
would make sense.

How much of my life has been a waste?
How many years and chances have I
wasted away and lost? And all this stuff
I'm just now beginning to figure out.
Why couldn't I have figured it all out as
a kid? Maybe I just wasn't smart enough
to. And it's just by luck now that I'm on
to this RAD thing in me.

* Really wanted to hoard (gorge) on the
sweets at the office today – like wanting
to hoard pens and those small note pads
(I LOVE those little note pads!).

I still hoard/stockpile things. Food, not
so much . . . but things. Like those sport
sunglasses. They don't make that model
anymore and I really liked that model.
And now they're gone! Forever.

STOCKPILE so you'll ALWAYS have it
(whatever the "it" may be). Especially
things now-a-days. They change the
style and come out with new models
while discontinuing the old ones all the
time. So, when you find a particular
style or size or model you really like
. . . STOCKPILE it b/c it will disappear
soon enough.

And it's only "stuff" . . . but I still feel
the need . . . it's almost (but not quite) a
compulsion. It's really a weird feeling
inside that won't settle down until you've
got "enough" of the "it" thing. Almost
sounds like a person who came through
the Great Depression of the 30s.

* I really am weird.

* It's "every man for himself" –

         not personal . . .

              just fact.

* Back to trauma stuff. If EVERYTHING,
or almost everything is seen/felt as a
traumatic event . . .

         THEN . . . ANYTHING . . . or almost

anything can be a TRIGGER to the traumatic event.

So A NEW event can be felt/seen as a NEW TRAUMA . . . <u>AND</u> be the TRIGGER for a PAST TRAUMATIC event . . .
AT THE SAME
TIME ! ! !

Which makes the PRESENT "TRAUMA" all that much MORE traumatic . . .

> Like a house of cards . . . one triggers another . . . which triggers another . . . and it all falls down.

* My thoughts on "shared traumatic events":

(1) IF a traumatic event is experienced by several people together as a group, the "weight" of that trauma is also "shared" to a certain extent. Like this:

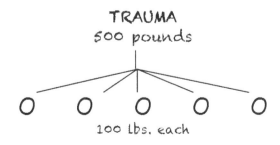

TRAUMA
500 pounds

100 lbs. each

Each person – in a sense – BEARS 100 pounds of the traumatic event as they deal with it collectively.

BUT . . .

(2) IF a traumatic event is experienced by one person ONLY . . . then that person – in a sense – BEARS all 500 pounds of the traumatic event. Like this:

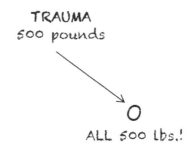

TRAUMA
500 pounds

ALL 500 lbs.!

(3) A person with RAD will still feel the whole burden of the event, even if others were present too, because since they are NOT CONNECTED to the "community" of the others, they don't feel the "shared load." Which only causes the RAD person to feel even MORE ISOLATED, ALONE, DIFFERENT and a "MISFIT" in society.

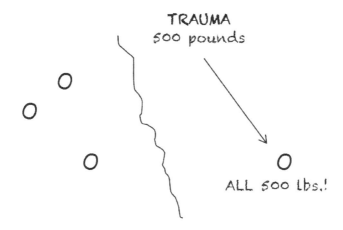

TRAUMA
500 pounds

ALL 500 lbs.!

NOT afraid of DYING at all. In fact, sometimes I wish for it. But I AM afraid of the PAIN and SUFFERING that comes before you actually die. I hope to die in my sleep so I don't have to deal with it coming. I don't mind dying . . . it's the suffering I DO mind.

* When other people die, what's my reaction (INWARDLY - because I KNOW what to do and how to look OUTWARDLY)?

I envy them . . .

and wish it were me.

I see them as the lucky One . . .

because they don't have to suffer anymore in this world.

And I wish I didn't have to suffer anymore either . . .

BUT NOOOOOO . . . not yet.

* Oh the feeling like a "misfit" in society is SCARY . . .

Because people usually attack what doesn't fit them . . .

The USs attack the THEMs and since I'm not a part of the US group . . . I'm a THEM and therefore a

Target = UNSAFE = RUN = SURVIVAL . . . AGAIN . . .

And YET . . . in all of this craziness . . . in the middle of the jungle war . . . raining . . . at night time . . . during a fire fight

THERE'S HOPE. WHY?

I don't exactly know <u>why</u>.

HOW?

I'm not entirely sure. That's why I'm journaling. To find the "how." I just know from living it and walking it all these years it's possible to get out of the jungle . . . to heal . . . move on . . . and practice at becoming a civilian – I don't think I'll ever be normal ("like it never happened") like everyone else . . . but maybe I can get normal enough to be at . . .

> PEACE . . . THAT'S what I want is PEACE. Non-combat, non-survival, non-"don't die" . . .

> PEACE . . . even if I have a scar (or several) and a limp . . . even if I have a couple of my knuckles that freeze up . . . to be at PEACE would be enough for me. Even if I don't "belong." To be at PEACE would be good enough.

* I want to tell the whole world "LEAVE ME ALONE!" "LET ME BE . . . @ PEACE!"

"PLEASE"

"DAMN IT!"

* The whole time I've been re-reading what I've written to this point, I've been chewing the inside of my lip - a TIC thing I have. Tried to stop any number of times and go back to it. Still working on stopping that particular TIC. We'll see . . .

* It was weird . . . I felt it this AM . . . Don't know what to call it except to call it "That Certain Pace/Mode" that I used to call "the drone mode." But it's a little different than that. This "pace" is a physical pace, speed, my body gets into - add to it a certain type mental "mode" (or something) and it activates the SURVIVAL PACE / THINKING / FEELING all over again. AND it's HARD to STOP it even when I recognize it. My body/ mind wanted to go back into that driven mode - or it felt more like I was being "pulled" back into that pace/mode. Really bazaar feeling. Almost like my being was on "auto-pilot" somehow. A robot mode with terror building inside at the same time. Terror that I won't get everything done that I need to . . . in the time I have . . . Had to consciously STOP over and over . . . consciously RELAX and RE-FOCUS. Then go back to doing things . . . weird. Very weird.

* I think I know why I like lists. I like to cross things out – almost "rub them out of existence" = it means SOMETHING IS OVER = DONE = CAN'T GO WRONG now . . . because it's "OVER." It's a relief that at least for that one thing nothing can get screwed up now . . .

* Reading through all I wrote last night and it seems so . . . SURFACE-ie . . . so "OVERVIEW" and lacking depth or lacking the "full" explanation. But, now that I think of it, that's what RAD is like a lot of the time – BECAUSE THERE IS NO TIME – to do things with "depth" or "completeness" or "_____."

My first reaction is to throw it all away and begin over (the ALL or NOTHING polarization again) . . . but I won't. Don't know exactly how I'll "go back" and "fill in the gaps" . . . we'll see. But it doesn't matter anyway. People will think I'm crazy weird . . . or something worse like a "monster" or something.

I'm bouncing all over the place here with my reading and research reading. Just finished the book "Saving Your Brain"[11] and here's my personal composite list from the whole of the book as to things that destroy brain cells.

* A cumulative list of things that can kill brain cells (causing brain damage):

Psychological inactivity
Physical inactivity
Head injury/Traumatic Brain Injury
Loss of teeth
Low education
PTSD *
Depression *
Excessive stress (especially when there's a low sense of control)
        Childhood traumas *
        Acute situations *
        Chronic situations *
Childhood sexual abuse
Anxiety *
Anger *
Low self-esteem *
Adrenalin reaction without a physical
        release *
Stressful workplace
        Insufficiently demanding
        Excessively demanding

Presence of chemical hazards
High demand but low control
Over-stimulation (inundated with sensory
    stimuli)
Hypertension/high blood pressure
Exposure to massive amounts of
    aluminum
Diabetes
Malnutrition

I marked all the ones directly
related to RAD with a * = 9 out of 19
items that a child could be exposed to.
That's about 1/2 of the list! Almost 50%
of the things that can damage a child's
brain are *directly related* to RAD.

OK . . . now I need to add the Head
Injuries piece – at least 3 of those
growing up. Went to the base hospital
for 2 of them and never told my parents
about the 3rd one. Head injuries are not
related to RAD . . . but according to the
author all these things are cumulative.

Oh, I also might as well add the sexual
abuse stuff. It's even hard to admit/
think about that stuff. Anyway. Again,
not "because" of RAD . . . but still gets
added onto the brain damage tally sheet.

No wonder I'm slow, stupid and don't get it ! ! 11 out of 19 things that can destroy brain cells in a child I've LIVED ! ! That's OVER 50% of things that can go wrong ... <u>DID</u> GO WRONG to my brain.

Hold on ... if RAD has "elements" (depression, anger, anxiety, etc.) that are EVERY DAY things in a RAD life ... then that makes sense that there is some ongoing brain destruction happening - even after the traumas stopped.

PLUS

    The Right-hemisphere NOT activated ...

        PLUS

            The Left-hemisphere NOT activated ...

YUCK!!

What's happening to the RAD person's GRAY MATTER ? Not the cognition part

of the brain . . . the MEDICAL,
NEUROLOGICAL, BIOLOGICAL part
of the brain ? ? ?

Does RAD cause PERMANENT BRAIN
DAMAGE ? ? ?

I don't know.

The author did also talk about things
that "create" new brain cells too. I put
together a cumulative list of those things
too. Here they are:

(next page)

A cumulative list of things that can save brain cells or rebuild brain cells:

Minimize workplace stress
     Balance demand/control
     Reduce hypertension-makers as
         much as possible
     Shift work
     Overtime work
     12-hour days
     Excessive noise
     Stay away from sexual harassment
     Get a job you enjoy
Minimize stress in overall lifestyle
Get help for depression
Get help for anxiety
Get help for anger
Get help for low self-esteem
Mindful meditation
Willful relaxation
Take necessary medications
     Depression
     PTSD
     Diabetes
     Hypertension
     Etc.
Get help for PTSD
Stay away from toxic chemicals as much
     as possible
Limit sensory stimulation to "sub-
     inundating" levels

Avoid a "dual career" situation for
     mothers as much as possible

"Possibly" –
     Estrogen Replacement Therapy for
          women
     Androgen Replacement Therapy for
          men
     1 "baby aspirin"/day
     Good potassium intake
     Dark chocolate in moderate amounts
     Tea in moderate amounts
     1 alcoholic beverage/week
     Vitamin E

Get diabetes and pre-diabetes under
     control
Maintain a healthy body weight
Good diet / good nutritional intake
Stay away from massive amounts of
     aluminum
Avoid smoking
Good calcium intake
Avoid head injuries
     Wear helmets
     Wear seatbelts
Regular, moderate amount of aerobic
     exercise
     Fast-paced walking is great
Raised in a good environment/
     experience as a child

Mentally active responses to cognitive
    challenges
    Learning new things
    Generating new ideas, etc.
    Teaching

Live life to the fullest

I have been doing some of those things
. . . at least lately . . . but . . .

      THE DAMAGE TO THE BRAIN . . .
* That (how ever much it was "quality"
wise) only ADDS to the feeling of NOT
being normal.

    "DIFFERENT"
    "MISFIT"

    (and now "BRAIN DAMAGED"
       too.)

See the web in all of this? How so many
things feed off other things which feed
the first things ? ? ? ?

* A BIG piece of the healing journey is

GETTING ORGANIZED.

Not "again" but for the first time EVER. Like this writing. Going back through all the pages and sorting out the ROE, tactics, polarization thinking, etc., etc., etc. and making sense and ORDER out of things – FOR THE 1st TIME EVER . . . is a HUGE part of the healing journey. And to see the WHAT actually happened, and the WHY, and the WHAT it did to me, and the WHY I'm doing it, thinking.

> To get the EXTERNAL organized it helps to "organize" my INTERNAL world; sweep and organize the garage, organize my closet, the bookshelves – the whole house basically.

There seems to be a CORRELATION between the INTERNAL and EXTERNAL worlds when it comes to being/feeling "organized" or "cluttered" or "scattered."

> (A) if the INTERNAL is "cluttered" and disorganized = my EXTERNAL world is probably disorganized and "out of sorts" too.

(B) to get INTERNALLY "organized" it helps to organize my EXTERNAL world. It's not a "magic fix" answer, but it's a great place to begin.

(C) if the EXTERNAL world is organized, it helps the INTERNAL world to feel more organized - or "less cluttered" as well.

* More . . .

NOT VERY "sentimental" @ all – Don't attach to things (either because they'll get taken away or broken).	"sentimental" – attach to one or to very few things (maybe an attempt to have at least "something").

How does the COGNITIVE belief "I'm not worthy" develop when the _____ ? _____ ___ was "decided upon" PRE – cognition (0 – 24 months)? Did the cognition "develop" as with other things "that's just the way the world is . . . as it IS"? Don't know.

So when doing Cognitive Behavioral Therapy work on "irrational beliefs" . . . or "stinking thinking" . . . or "faulty

perceptions" – remember that you're
dealing with BOTH

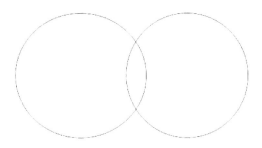

5 year old child who "made"
that belief and all the
emotional charge tied to it.
Or the infant maybe . . .

The middle-aged person now
who is sitting across the room
from you now

THIS "ONE" (part of the brain)
only understands
EXPERIENTIAL
Realities will be emotionally
driven/charged. A "concrete
thinker" only

THIS "ONE" (part of the brain)
can understand logic
Cognitive reasoning, etc.
and can keep the emotions
more in check. An "abstract
thinker".

And when it comes to the "Why, God?" questions . . . you're dealing with

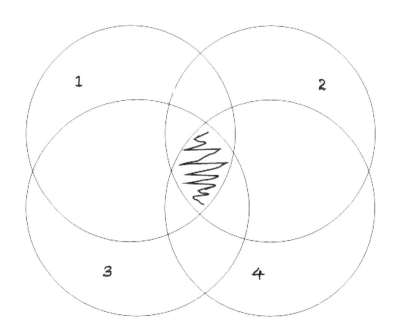

You have a:

(1) 5 year old + spiritual questions
(2) 5 year old + concrete questions
(3) grown person + spiritual questions
(4) grown person + abstract questions.
You NEED to "ANSWER" THE QUESTIONS ON ALL 4 CIRCLES /
        Overlapping areas . . .
            Before the "answers" can be
                "ACCEPTED" into the
system and begin – BEGIN – being
    used.

Maybe this is true for most or all of the "Cognitive Disorders" a RAD person has to work through. And what – I'm guessing here – might throw a therapist if they're not seeing the "5 year old" side of the diagram.

Even if it's not a specifically "spiritual" topic . . . "spirituality" stuff is there somewhere most likely.

* THE BIG TIRED hits. A HUGE, bigger than life, tired beyond tired which is beyond all exhaustion . . . A HUGE "WHUMP!"

> The HUGE "LET DOWN" that comes after you can FINALLY stop running / hiding / fighting after all those years. The "COLLAPES" after the SHOCK wears off . . . FINALLY . . .

>> The big "let down" after the trauma that you had to keep your head about you ends.

THE ACCUMULATIVE IMPACT OF ALL THE IMPACT IN YOUR LIFE . . .

THE IMPACT OF BEING "OVER THE TOP"
EXHAUSTED BECAUSE OF LIVING IN
SURVIVAL MODE FOR HOW MANY YEARS ! !

It's physical . . .

it's emotional . . .

it's "spiritual" . . .

EXHAUSTION beyond words or
comprehension. And it takes
several MONTHS to a YEAR to
grow out of the tiredness.

The only real thing I could do was REST
and RELAX as much as I could and as
often as I could. A sabbatical in the
Bahamas would have been nice . . . but
it didn't happen. So basically I worked,
came home got dinner, and went to bed.
I don't know what I would have done if
I'd been raising a child or having to care
for an ailing parent. It was "enough"
just to handle me.

You work when you have to . . .
and . . .

You rest the remainder of the
time as you can . . .

month after month
after month . . . until
when?

Until you're not tired anymore from "surviving."

How long is that? Don't know . . . "Until you're not tired anymore" is the best answer I can give. It all depends on the battles and how many. Remember = it will take 2 YEARS or so for the hormone levels to settle down to a "normal" level for stress. So the BIG TIRED will take a while too. NO DOUBT.

* "All's fair in love and war." And this is WAR . . . so . . . ALL REALLY IS FAIR . . .

WHATEVER KEEPS ME FROM "DYING" IN THE MOMENT IS . . . "FAIR" . . .

"OK" . . .

"RIGHT."

* RAD can "mix" with - or be "hidden" behind any number of legitimate diagnoses:

* in kids –
  ADD / ADHD
  Developmental delays
  Processing disorders
  Learning disabilities
  Anxiety
  Separation anxiety
  Depression
  PTSD
  "Slow learner"
  "Lazy"
  Oppositional Defiant (ODD)
  Eating Disorders
  Asperger's Syndrome
  Conduct Disorder
  "Strong Willed Child" ("on
        steroids")
  Obsessive Compulsive
        Disorder
  Anger management issues
  Sexually promiscuous /
        acting out
  Compulsive lying
  Violent / aggressive
        behaviors
  Kleptomania
  Sleep disorders

* in adults –
    ADD / ADHD
    Developmental delays
    Processing disorders
    Learning disabilities
    Anxiety
    Depression
    PTSD
    "Lazy"
    Oppositional Defiant (ODD)
    Eating Disorders
    Asperger's Syndrome – you
        don't outgrow it
    Obsessive Compulsive
        Disorder
    Anger management issues
    Sexually promiscuous/acting
        out
    Compulsive lying
    Violent/aggressive behaviors
    Kleptomania
    Sleep disorders
    "Relationship problems" in
        marriage, etc.
    Chemical dependency or
        addictions in general
    "Self centered"
    Personality disorders =
        Narcissism
        Borderline
        Anti-social

Histrionic
Avoidant
Schizotypal
Schizoid
Obsessive Compulsive
(OCPD)
"Personality disorder
NOS"
Chronic fatigue syndrome
Domestic violence
perpetrator
"Perfectionistic"
"Control freak"
Etc., etc., etc.

BUT . . . UNDERNEATH all these legitimate diagnosable disorders – I realized as I was making the list, not all are official "disorders" – is . . . or COULD BE . . .

RAD . . . diagnosed or not.

Or at least the traits of RAD.

So . . . when it comes to TREATMENT PLAN time for a RAD person . . . you have to deal with . . .

Depression + RAD
Anxiety + RAD
Addiction + RAD

Personality disorder + RAD
Eating disorder + RAD
Personality disorder + addiction + RAD

and it can pile up into a MULTI-LAYER pile of "stuff" to psychologically work on.

For me:

RAD + depression + anxiety + anger issues + PTSD + perfectionism + brain damage stuff + sexual abuse + sleep "issues" (no official disorder though) + OCPD (at least the traits of it).

=

ONE HELL OF A "JOURNEY" for me and Sandy!

Yuck ! ! ! Just writing out that "formula" makes me sick! And angry too ! ! Because it wasn't my fault. At least most of it wasn't my doing. But the "perfectionism" was my only option . . . so I don't know really how much of a "choice" I had in that one either.

AAAUGGGGGGG !

* So why would ANYBODY in their right mind sign up to work with somebody like me? I'm glad she did. YUCK . . . God bless her!

But I still don't know why anyone would WILLINGLY sign up for "journeys" like this. And I don't know of ANYBODY who would WILLINGLY sign up to marry somebody like this! I sure would NOT marry the likes of me. Now that I know what I know. Before, I thought I was a "great catch." But now . . . I'm a "stay away from" person.

* I think I'm in my 2nd year of the BIG TIRED – and I'm STILL tired most of the time. I NEED to rest (not "sleep" all the time) until 10:00am today before getting out of bed. Made myself get up and get to work – too bad it wasn't the weekend yet.

I MADE myself get up and go to work – because I CHOOSE to . . . not because I "HAD" to. That's a shift in me too; choosing to do things not b/c I "have" to only. But I could most definitely use more hours of rest.

The FRIEND or FOE question – or

polarization – isn't really "FRIEND" . . . It's more a "beneficiary" ("Can I 'benefit' from you?" If "yes" = "friend") not a true "friend" person.

* Polarized thinking:

MINIMIZE	CATASTROPHIZE
(Not dead yet = I'm OK)	("Do" or "Die!")
"Last man standing" = "thanks"	Can't let another person get hurt because of me

Jesus' death for me . . .

Does not compute . . . It jams my brain. I get the Concept / theology . . . but it does NOT compute.

NO TIME!	HAVE to do "it" "perfectly", completely "right" the first time
NO TIME waiting	Always waiting . . . waiting . . . waiting . . .

* A hard "reality" to learn for RAD is that PAIN IS <u>NOT THE</u> ENEMY – or at least PAIN (#1) (see prior notes).

* It's weird that . . . why NOW am I remembering things from when I was a child? I mean, not remembering very much at all of the first 10 or so years of my life should have been a clue to "something" not being "normal," but why now? Maybe it's because of all the journaling and reading on all this stuff. Don't know. But I guess that's not uncommon though for RAD.

* I forgot to include the added dimensions of chronic PHYSICAL pain that adds complications to the RAD situation = makes it PHYSICALLY a "fight or flight" survival mode as well as an emotional one.

* Don't like crowds, big groups, social parties . . . I feel the "trapped" or "hemmed in" feeling . . . YUCK . . .

* A word picture came to mind yesterday – the "FIRE" of/for =

  living – wanting – loving – existing

has been smothered out. There's nothing but ashes and cold embers . . .

BUT . . . somewhere at the bottom of all the cold moist embers is 1 or 2 very small coals with a very little bit of spark still left in them. The HEALING process is a lot like GENTLY finding – and uncovering – and GENTLY fanning that faint spark or two. Then ADDING "burnable" substance . . . BIT by BIT . . . SLOWLY and CAREFULLY. NURSING the spark alive again into a fire for living and wanting and loving and existing.

(If you "over do it" – or try too hard or too fast – you can put the last spark out all together . . . most likely "forever" . . .)

BE VERY CAREFUL !

THAT'S how "broken" and "on the edge" of dying it feels like inside.

I can remember thinking of dying a LOT of the time as a kid. It was always "dying with honor in battle" or some variation of that. And I can remember

– this is weird – feeling a smile coming over me when I thought of myself actually being dead. That's strange for a kid to daydream that much about something like that. Hummmmmmm . . .

I often wish I'd die in my sleep.

* I can remember the "box" I "built" around me as a child. Old left over planks – the 1 x 4 types – and a hastily made "crate" to hide the "little me" in.

> To protect that part of me from being hurt ever again.
> To keep everyone away from "getting to me."

The picture is still clear – about 4 or 5 years old maybe – maybe 24" high on each side with a top covering it all. Not big, but just big enough to scrunch down in and hide. It was dark inside too. I built it to shut the world and everybody out. I realize – now – that the crate also shut God out as well – without realizing it, the "trust NOBODY" also included God.

later a picture came to me showing God's hand handing the boards to me –

HELPING me box myself away. It was His "survival tactics" He put in me that I was accessing . . . He gave me the boards that He knew I would use to shut Him out as well. Knowing that He and I would need to revisit this crate years later and let the "inner child" out of the box.

This is verrrrrrrry weird. Don't think I'll be telling Sandy this any time soon that's for sure.

Whatever we use to hide our "inner child" in will NOT be fancy or well stocked – THAT would draw attention to it and it could be found. It's HIDDEN in the "junk heap" . . . it looks very UN – VALUABLE so nobody will even go near it . . . it's UN-INVITING so as to not even get noticed . . . and it's "empty" inside (not "stocked" with supplies) b/c there weren't any supplies to get our hands on in the first place – not "enough."

And it's usually HIDDEN or BURIED . . .

DEEP . . .
VERY DEEP . . .
inside.

Usually in a dark, damp, cold, "unfriendly" place – just how "everyday" felt the day I hid myself there.

Oh . . . and along the way, I've put booby traps and "destruction"
around to MAKE SURE NOBODY . . . EVER . . . finds the box.

EVEN ME . . .

MO = "don't die" = can't find that "me" . . . ever . . . and if the "me" can't be found . . . then it can't be killed . . . and I "don't die."

"Finding" that "me" . . .

* Stop . . . I just remembered playing "hide and seek" as a little, little kid. I wasn't playing the "game" with friends – there were no friends – I was trying to "hide" from the whole world. One time Mother spent "hours" (in her words) looking for me, even had the MPs come looking too, to find me. And I was in a small box in the storage unit all the base housing had back in those days. I think if my memory is correct, I fell asleep in the box before finally an MP found me. Man was he angry! And boy did Mother light into me when everybody finally left the house.

She beat me really bad. Bad enough I was hoping it would kill me - then it would all be over . . . finally. That was the moment I vowed never to cry . . . ever again. And I didn't that day which only made Mother more crazed and she beat me even more - trying to get me to cry. Never did. But was hoping she'd just do it a little more so I could finally die.

That's morbid . . . I mean LITERALLY. That's NOT normal child thinking. But you'd never know by looking at or talking with me today.

Back to the "finding me" . . . Finding that "me" is = to dying because that part is so fragile that 1 more thing will kill me. So to "ensure" I "won't die" I have to ensure that box, with me in it, will NEVER BE FOUND . . .

        HIDDEN = NOT DIE
        FOUND = DIE NOW

I CANNOT let it be FOUND . . . EVER . . . EVER . . . EVER . . .

        (even by me).

So you hear the RISK involved in letting myself get close enough to that box to deal with its "contents" = "me"? Its like VOLUNTEERING to die and renounce my MO!! It's even more TERRORIZING than the TERROR I feel every day already.

* The concept of TIME is just that . . . a CONCEPT . . . it's not a REALITY . . . it's not CONCRETE . . .

> Dark / light is REAL
> Blonde hair / no hair is REAL

And since RAD has no real "object permanence" there can be no REAL SENSE (or CONCEPT) of HAVING TIME . . .

> That's why it's always NOT . . .
> TOO LATE . . .
> OVER . . .
> or WAITING . . .

THOSE are CONCRETE . . . THOSE are REAL / TANGIBLE realities.

And that's all RAD has to go on in relationship to this TIME concept. That's why - I'm sure even though I can't "empirically prove" it - RAD has a hard time with "CAUSE AND EFFECT" THINKING.

It's a CONCEPT . . .

when THIS happens . . .

THEN . . . sometime later
(whenever "later" is) . . .

THIS will happen as a direct
result of the "former"
(whatever the "earlier" is)
thing, action, choice.

Cause and Effect ONLY "works" – if
understood – when the person has a
sense (concept) of: TIME . . .
SEQUENCE
ORDER . . .

RAD HAS NO SENSE of any of these 3
concepts . . .

But . . . like any lab rat can figure a
problem out by conditioning and luck
. . . RAD does learn to do / not do based
upon painful conditioning and the HUGE
desire to AVOID PAIN @ ALL COSTS !

But that's NOT the same as "cause and
effect" thinking process – which, by the

way, is more of a left brain hemisphere function. And RAD doesn't have much of that going on. So NO WONDER there's a LACK of cause and effect thinking in us as children, teens and even adults.

It's not that we're stupid or slow or "defiant" or not paying attention or not trying . . . the part of the brain that "does that stuff" = CAUSE AND EFFECT THINKING . . . is NOT WORKING . . . and NOT ABLE to work ! !

* Talk about a set up for childhood learning disabilities! Is the RAD kid damned or what?!
And if all you do is address the "LD" . . . you'll miss the REAL ISSUE. My brain isn't "turned on" there . . . because the "survival" part of my brain is doing all the "work" . . .

And I'll get labeled as uncooperative and incorrigible b/c I'm not "trying" or "taking advantage of the opportunities given to me" or some dumb thing like that.

OK . . . to be fair to all my teachers - especially the elementary school ones - it wasn't their fault they didn't identify it. Who would have thought "the son of a Naval Aviator who's Mother is involved in everything" would be RAD?

And I don't know if they even knew about RAD back in those days. It just happened that way.

But NOBODY . . . EVER . . . QUESTIONED "Maybe there's something more deeply wrong with this boy" and bothered to look deeper! !

NOBODY ! ! ! ! !

But . . . camouflage . . . how COULD they have questioned b/c I did my best to hide it and look as "normal" as I could.

It wasn't anybody's fault.

Wait . . . it WAS somebody's fault . . . it was my PARENTS' fault ! . . . they made the environment be like war in the jungle for their young son.

I REFUSE to do the psychological "blame the parents" thing. How stupid.

They dealt me my hand of cards . . .

It's been up to me to play my
cards as best as I can . . . whether
the game is Hearts, Spades
or Poker.

But . . . somewhere here doesn't some of
the TRUTHFULNESS need to land on them?

I don't know. That scrambles my brain
just to think about it.

* Another "formula" thing to follow:

NO "object permanence"

+

NO "trust" in anything/ anybody

+

NO sense of "safe"

+

NO "time"

=

NO HOPE (REALLY) ! !

Think about it.

Hope in WHAT ???

> That it will get better in the "future?"
> That it will be "over" soon???
> That it will "get better" at all?

> That I'll get to "home base?"
> (because there is NO "home base").

What is there to hope IN?

> NOTHING REALLY . . . except
that maybe (if I'm lucky) I won't have to
wake up tomorrow to the "same ole
. . . same ole . . . same ole . . ." (survival
mode).

So for a person to KEEP GOING there
HAS to be HOPE in SOMETHING . . . RAD

puts its "hope" in:

> (1) I'll figure it out somehow and won't be hurt anymore (control)
> (2) maybe I won't wake up tomorrow (no such luck . . .)
> (3) I'll figure out how to be perfect (good enough) that THIS will make all the crap be over with.

* See why the <u>lucky</u> ones died ? ?

* Now ADD a PTSD "flashback" or "ab-reaction" into the "formula" mix I wrote out above:

NO object permanence
NO safe
NO trust
+ NO time

---

and what do you have?

BIG TIME CONFUSION ! !

What's REALLY real now?

What's NOT real now?

How can I tell the 2 apart (the "then" from the "now")?

Are they separate events anyway . . . really?

What was "then" and what is "now" really?

How do I know if there's any difference between "then" and "now"?

How can I "trust" my own senses?

How can I "trust" my own thinking?

How can I "trust" ME?

And . . . If I can't even depend on (trust) ME . . . to tell me what's REAL now or not . . . then I have NO ONE to TRUST to tell me the TRUTH and/or look out for me . . . even ME . . . I can't even trust myself . . . then how will I EVER know what's REAL – NOW – or not???

* A flashback = CONFUSION
                LOSS OF CONTACT with
                    reality
                    A high possibility for
            "paranoia" (for sure!)

DAHA ! ! That's SO obvious . . . "losing connectedness with reality" in the form of hallucinations, delusions, voices, sounds, flashbacks, nightmares, etc.

HELLO ! ! !
I'm NOT CRAZY ...

I'm being MADE crazy by all of this!!

And getting stuck in the middle of one of these flashbacks (or nightmares if you're asleep) FEELS CRAZY!!! It really does.

Sandy is good at telling me "you're NOT crazy. It just FEELS crazy!"

Sometimes I can believe that . . . sometimes it's a chore to believe.

* To anybody who cares . . .

RAD + PTSD = HELL ON EARTH ! !

* That SAFE acrostic has changed during all this healing process to:

S = solidly grounded
A = assertive
F = friendship
E = exercising healthy level of
       control

* BUT . . . it has taken a LONG TIME and a LOT of HARD WORK . . . to get this far. FEELING the safe is still an ongoing process . . . even now . . .

THAT'S why I DO need HELP . . . and am AFRAID of it at the same time . . . because you'll find out just how crazy I REALLY am . . . and you'll HURT me with that information by "locking me up" or . . .

Calling me crazy - and treating me that way. We do as a society treat the "crazy person" very differently . . . and try as we may (if we try at all) we don't do a good job of hiding our real feelings.

> Belittling me (all in "gest" of course)
> Talk behind my back - and tells
>   others I'm crazy
> Label me somehow - and block a
>   promotion or something
> Try to take my "rights" away from
>   me legally so you can "choose"
>   for me what kind of medical
> procedures happen to me, where
> I can live, etc.

> Or . . . or . . . or . . . or . . .

HELP
(me)

DO NOT
COME
CLOSE TO
ME!

* Again, writing this stuff sounds
awful! And it is . . . but yet, it isn't at
the same time. I don't consider myself
a "bad person" and I doubt anybody at
work would think that either. This is the
"private war" that's storming inside. And
while it's a "war" and it's "storming" . . .
(this will be weird to say) . . . it doesn't
feel all that bad. I mean, I do my job.
I'm friendly to the neighbors and the
folks at church. I keep my road rage
INSIDE the car and never (never) let it
come out onto other drivers. I keep my
house clean. I provided as a husband
and as a father - when they were here.

I also have a feeling that "Yes, I have my
own quirks like everybody does, but
other than that, I'm an ok guy."

I know I'm not totally "normal" but I
feel closer to "normal" than I do to
"monster."

Again . . . no words ! !

* The reason RAD can't do "PEOPLE" or "FAMILY"
    24 / 7 – or even "very much" – is because –
    HUMAN = HURT which means, whenever I'm around people (for any reason) it's a "war zone" to me.

I can do OK when it's a planned function or activity or there's a planned purpose for our meeting – I still don't like too much of it, but it's OK.

I CAN *INTERACT*

What's NOT OK is to be around people with no plan or agenda – the socializing or relating stuff. During an official meeting I at least know the purpose and what's expected of me – so I KNOW HOW TO INTERACT.

When it's a social / "INFORMAL" type of setting, I DON'T KNOW what to expect or how to respond.

I CAN'T *RELATE*

THAT = BIG, HUGE "out of control" feeling and "Alpha Alert" sirens go off inside my entire being.

That's why I like NATURE / the out-of-doors so much. I realize some RAD people may be terrified of the wilderness because to them it = "out of control."

But to me it = IN CONTROL.

Why?

Because nature does what nature is going to do. It IS predictable, unlike human beings. You just need to LEARN/KNOW and work with nature.

* Nature does NOT play "favorites" because of wealth, position, rank, status, or any other factor that people can show partiality over. If it's going to snow, it will snow . . . no matter:

> Who you are
> How much $$ you have or don't have
> Whether you're skin is black, white, yellow or sunburned
> Whether you're a skilled outdoorsman or not
> Whether you're an Ensign or an Admiral

Whether you want it to snow or
   not
Whether you're mafia or
   law-abiding citizen
Whether you're an atheist,
   Buddhist, Christian or
   Muslim
Whether you're smart or dumb –
   the dumb may get you
   killed when it snows, but it
   doesn't "bring on" or "stop"
   the snow from falling
Whether you're male or female
Whether you're young or old

   . . . IT WILL SNOW.
* Nature/the wilderness is NOT A
"RESPECTOR OF PERSONS" . . .
   IT TREATS EVERY PERSON THE SAME –

A far cry from how humans treat each
other!! Even the wild animals will
behave like wild animals do – they
are not "respecters of persons" either.
Bears will do what bears do.

And it sort of is like a jungle war in some ways too:

> play by IT'S RULES ONLY . . . or
>   you'll die . . .
> is NEVER out to "punish" or "make you suffer"
> it's not PERSONAL, is NEVER a "respecter of persons" – not really . . . the faster you learn ITS WAYS the better chance you have of "not dying" . . .
> there is no GUARENTEE that you'll "not die" . . . even if you do DO EVERYTHING "by their rules" . . .
> ANY mistake could be the FATAL one . . . . if it was NOT you really got lucky . . . but don't count on being lucky again you can't afford to make a "mistake"
> . . . neither are "merciful"
> . . . neither are out to get you
> both will continue on even after you die . . .
> you can't "conquer" them . . .
> you can only "cooperate" with them . . .

240

* The RAD way of viewing interaction with another person:

"I have 'limited' resources and there isn't much of 'me' left either"	"You're trying to TAKE AWAY from me (my limited resources) or TAKE some of 'me' AWAY from me"
MO = "Don't die!"	BOTH = HURT = "die" *For your benefit* AT MY EXPENSE ! !
"So keep/hoard/hide my 'limited' resources and hide 'me' so 'me' doesn't get pulled apart and 'die'".	"RUN . . . baby . . .RUN!" "NO!"

I never truly saw it as FREELY GIVING to them . . .

It was always THEM TAKING from me.

And there is some truth to that. People often DO "take" from me:

Maybe FOR their own benefit

AND there is a COST to me of some sort . . . often BUT . . . follow the thinking here . . . .

ANY COST is a COST TOO GREAT in an "ALL or NOTHING" world.

ANY COST is a COST TOO HIGH TO PAY.

AND besides . . . I really DON'T have anything of value to "give" to you anyway — so they just want to hurt/use me for their own personal benefit . . .

which means YOU'RE NOT SAFE TO BE AROUND

LATE = "in trouble" = PAIN
      = "missed out" = PAIN in the
        form of loss
      = "bad thing" = "your fault" =
        PAIN

To AVOID POTENTIAL PAIN = ARRIVE EARLY . . . scope things out and make sure "the coast is clear."

EARLY = not "in trouble"
      = didn't "missed out"
      = got a chance to "scope things

out" to know what will be expected of me, how to "do" whatever will need to be "done" so I get it "right" the first time.
= use to the waiting anyway
= if somebody needs to "suffer" by "waiting" it's better for it to be me (since I'm less valuable than you)

But . . . but . . . but . . . that (above) is a contradiction/polarization to the having no concept of TIME and "Cause and Effect thinking." Hear it?

And the "being late" thing can be a control tactic too to keep you off guard and to show that I'm really in control of when this meeting (or whatever) begins.
I'm guessing, it's EITHER . . . OR . . .

A RAD person, just my guess here, will more times than not BE LATE – chronically. For the few like me who have some of those perfectionistic and OCD traits . . . we'll end up being EARLY most, if not all, of the time.

* I could see a person with the Narcissistic or Histrionic or Borderline Personality Disorders being the LATE ones because they want everybody to notice their entrance and give acknowledgement to them. Just my guess. Probably RAD people with legitimate ADD/ADHD would be LATE too.

Those RAD people with Dependent or Schizoid or Obsessive Compulsive Personality Disorders may tend to be the EARLY ones. Again, just my guess.

* I found this "quiz" for teens and/or adults as a PRIMER INQUIRY as to whether they may have attachment issues or not:

OOPS . . . next page.

ATTACHMENT PRIMER QUIZ[12]

Do you ...

1. Have a hard time genuinely trusting others
2. Feel anger that seems out of proportion to the situation
3. Feel uncomfortable when you're "tied down" or "locked in" to a commitment
4. Have low self-esteem
5. Have a hard time making cause-and-effect connections
6. Feel like you're in "survival mode" a lot of the time
7. Have a fear of withdrawal of support (or you walk away first, to get the "being left" over with on your terms)
8. Have to know what's coming at you ahead of time
9. Dislike unexpected noise
10. Fear being manipulated, controlled or taken advantage of
11. Fear being deprived of certain possessions – valuable or sentimental
12. Dislike being held, touched or hugged without your consent
13. Have a dislike for environments where there seems to be no one in charge (or any "out of control" situation)
14. Dislike being left alone (really)
15. Have a high threshold for discomfort and/or pain
16. Demand affection on your terms
17. Lack genuinely deep relationships

18. Have a strong need to be in control
    (directly or indirectly)
19. Have feelings of anxiety
20. Engage in self-critical thinking regularly
21. Often feel "different"
22. Have bouts of depression
23. Tend to be hyperactive and/or
    hypersensitive
24. Feel apprehensive a lot of the time
25. Pride yourself in being self-sufficient

This is a partial list of symptoms that describe what's known as Reactive Attachment Disorder. If you circled 10 or more items, it's likely you have some attachment issues. Check it out.

Took the quiz and I scored 19 out of the 25 possible questions. Think I may have some "attachment issues?"

* Realized just yesterday that I have a HOME. It's never been "home" before. It's just been "the house" . . . and sometimes "my house" . . . but never a "home" or as a kid (as far as I can remember with this faulty remembering I have) or as an adult. Even when I was married it wasn't our "home" . . . it was just "the house."

That change has occurred over time and I'm sure maybe a part of my not wanting to ever call it a "home" is b/c I didn't want to "attach" to a place either.

"Home is where your rump rests!" and that's good enough for me.

That has also GOT to be a military brat thing too – a TCK (Third Culture Kid) thing as they call it now. So, I don't think it is entirely a RAD thing . . . but one compounds the other =

    RAD + TCK = "no home" . . . no "roots" . . . no "home base" to "go back to."

The TCK thing can give that "wander lust" sensation. I can remember never throwing any boxes away. We collapsed all the "savable" boxes and stored them – and saved the unused packing tape – because we knew we'd be moving in 2 years. It still kind of feels weird NOT to pack up and move every 2 years or so. And the TCK stuff mentions that. Oh well . . . just another "piece to the puzzle" here.

But it feels "not normal" to call this place "home." It feels weird and good at the same time. And the mix of those

2 things feels weird. It's just strange.
Anyway . . .

* That DRONE MODE is a mix of:

> (1) mindset of anxiousness over
> getting somewhere "on time" or
> getting things done "in time"
> PLUS
> (2) a certain body pace/rhythm
> - even my steps fall into a certain
> cadence
> THEN
> (3) the eyes become "singularly
> focused" as does the mind
> (4) body tenses up and EVERY part
> of me gets "into the rhythm."

I think people - non-RAD people - may
be able to understand RAD - at least
MORE then I thought. Some people will
be able to "get it" at least enough to help
and be positively empathetic. That's good
- it FEELS good that others can
understand me at least to some extent
- maybe not 100% experientially - but
that's OK . . . people can "get it" more
- and maybe a LOT MORE . . .

BUT they have to be willing to listen and
listen and not try it fit into what they

"already understand." They'll have to "think outside the box" b/c this is truly a "different" box all together.

So maybe . . .

* There really ARE NOT words that can adequately describe the "BIG TIRED" . . .

It's like –

BODY
MIND
HEART
SOUL . . . are ALL a deep tired
beyond "tired" all at the
same time.

"The deepest expression of any emotion is silence." I can't find who said that. UFFFGGGG.

So when/if I finally DO "get it" that it was NOT my fault . . . 2 things happen:

(1) the middle-aged adult in me = RAGES at the injustice and wrong and sickness of it all ! !!

(2) the "inner child"/5year old "me" = TOTAL TERRROR because there IS no control . . . no being able to "fix" it after all. No place to HIDE, NOTHING to be said or done to change the outcome. NOTHING'S the same either.

TOTAL POWERLESSNESS
TOTAL HELPLESSNESS
TOTAL "NAKEDNESS"

TOTAL TERROR

You'd think it'd be a relief to finally see it wasn't my fault. But it's not. It has to some, I know that much (the adult part of me) . . . but . . .

And yes, eventually the "inner child" did get in touch with the RAGE inside – but only when the adult was willing and able and could "secure safety" while he RAGED and RAGED and RAGED.

But I don't seem to stay long in the RAGE because it's like this; RAGE is a small sliver of the continuum. Like this:

TOTAL TERROR

RAGE (sometimes even missing)

GRIEF, SADNESS, PAIN, LOSS

As an adult I may stay in the RAGE for some time, because I "know" how WRONG it was – FINALLY.

The "inner child" (sounds so therapeutic doesn't it?) is so BROKEN that the PAIN takes over everything.

It FEELS like I've written SO Much (quality not content).	It FEELS like I've written SO Little (really – quality, Content, or quantity).

This whole idea of "discovering" what SAFE is, is sort of like trying to put together a jigsaw puzzle where =

> you don't know the puzzle's finished size
> you don't know its final shape
> you don't know the number if pieces
> and you don't have the box top to know what the "picture" is
> . . . all having been dropped from a 10 story window to the ground
> . . . in a wind storm!

How's that for a word picture? I do like it. It describes it well.

Will probably need to make this an ongoing list:

PIECES OF THE "SAFE" PUZZLE

(1) Time – you have time now, not everything is "NOW or DIE."

(2) "Safe" is always in the present moment (not the future). I want to be SURE I'll NEVER be hurt again . . . ever and since I can't control the future I walk right by the SAFE that IS here IN THE PRESENT MOMENT.

(3) Is worth the risk to look for and begin to hope for. But it's still a risk to expect / hope / want / desire (because you'll only get your hopes dashed and it will hurt more).

(4) Being SAFE is STILL important . . . NEVER give up SAFE . . . just need to change:

   (a) definition of SAFE (more than

likely) and
(b) tactics we use to try and get
safety. This goes back to my
acrostics I wrote out earlier on
SAFE and how they changed.
Changing the tactics is also
changing the ROE.

(5) The ability (experientially) to separate
the "2 Kinds of Pain" I wrote about
before.

(6) You have options/choice . . . you
really do . . . and you do all the time.
Even if you don't like your collection of
choices . . . you still have a choice. It's
not a "have to" . . . it's a CHOICE now.
This is a HUGE piece.

(7) Healthy cognitions is a HUGE piece of
SAFE too! Which is this list, in a way.

(8) "Both-And" thinking replaces the
"Either-Or" thinking. Again a HUGE
cognition shift.

(9) Realizing I don't have to know
EVERYTHING before being SAFE. This is
one of those cognitive reality statements.

(10) Accepting the REALITY that there is no FUTURE guarantee ... AND ... I can STILL be SAFE right now ... BOTH.

(11) Some kind of HEALTHY interaction with at least 1 other human being. This may START with a "safe" and attaching relationship with a pet. Eventually, it may spread to humans. Pets seem to be more unconditional with their love than many humans – even healthy ones.

Moving from INTERACTING to RELATING to ATTACHING is a slow and DELIBERATE choice to make and work on. Pets seem less threatening too so maybe start there if relating to a human being feels like too much of a stretch.

(12) QUIET does NOT = pain / bad / being punished. Quiet is just ... quiet and it's OK. And sometimes it's good to "choose" times of quiet on the OUTSIDE so the INSIDES can begin to quiet down. But so often quiet was equated with rejection or abandonment which = pain.

(13)

* A RAD person can easily see others as:
    (1) irresponsible

(2) incompetent

. . . because they take life too "lightly" – not like it's "do or die" serious

because to me, seeing things in a "do or die" seriousness is "normal" . . .

therefore it's being –

responsible and competent.

So anything less than "normal" IS . . .

IN-competent
and
IR-responsible . . .
that's what makes sense to me.

And it's ONE MORE reason not to TRUST other people either . . .

because their "incompetent-ness" and their "irresponsibility" may HURT ME! !!

* RAD has to learn that "normal" is in relation to their bodies – sickness, pain, injuries, etc. I don't know what "level of pain" needs what "level of care." What

deserves an Aspirin? What deserves stitches? What deserves a trip to the ER?

The old RAD thinking was "If I'm not dead . . . I'm OK."

I see – now – that that isn't healthy thinking, NOR was it really SAFE either. So part of the healing process, and a "piece of the SAFE puzzle," is to learn – via experience and feedback – what level of pain deserves what level of treatment.

What makes this learning SAFE even harder is the added impact of PTSD and DISSOCIATION (which I understand by the grid thing not all RAD people have)?

A person who has no clue on what level of pain deserves which level of treatment and what's the difference between PAIN #1 (when I dislocated my finger) and PAIN #2 (when I broke my hand).

In learning this balance, others will likely observe (those close enough to) "normal" reactions for a CHILD of:

(1) OVER - reacting to a pain

and then / or next time

(2) UNDER - reacting to a pain.

This UP and DOWN reacting is a normal experiential learning process for a child when they are learning to understand that balance between injury and treatment. But when it's being learned by an adult - and displayed in an adult - people are far less tolerant/ sympathetic and less understanding too. Which makes sense, but it doesn't help the learning process and tends to re-validate the "I'm weird, different, the outcast" thinking.

* Another "formula" –

"People are generally irresponsible and incompetent."
+
"Don't/can't trust anybody.
+
"Every man for himself."
+
"I can handle more pain/suffering than other people can" (which is likely true).
+
* Little or no empathy (really) for others and an overall lack of any caring emotion that's able to come out.
+
Naturally suspicious and hyper-vigilant.
+
Having to be "RIGHT" (because if I'm NOT "right" . . . I'll get hurt.). And even if I'm NOT right . . . I have to be "right" or else I DESERVE to be hurt even if hurt didn't naturally come.
+   (to be continued ...) Ha
An intensity in life to do things "right" and "perfect."
=
AND WHAT DOES THAT LOOK LIKE TO OTHERS AROUND? What does it add up to?

Aloof
"Holier than thou"
Arrogant
Selfish
Self-centered
Judgmental
Condescending
Narcissistic
"Too good for the rest of us"
"Goodie-2-shoes"
Perfect
Always trying to be "Mr. Right"
Know-it-all
Controlling
Passive / aggressive
"Pushy"
Bossy
Unpredictable
"Loose cannon"
OCD
Exocentric
Paranoid
Not a "team player"
"Off in his own world"
Intimidating
Melodramatic

I've been called most of these things at some point in time. And . . . I probably WAS . . . now that I look back on it. But I wasn't TRYING to be those things. But

when you "add up" the tally sheet . . .
what are you going to get?

For me it's not that I WANTED or TRIED
to be any of those things. I meant no
harm to anybody else. It's just that
THAT'S THE WAY MY WORLD IS/WAS . . .
again, it's not personal
and there was no harm intended
. . .

But . . . it IS "last man
standing" . . .and that "last man"
is going to be me.

It *has* to be me . . . my MO
is "Not die."

And I can see how a RAD person would
"develop" into a:

Narcissist
Domestic Violence perpetrator
Socio-path
Borderline
OCPD
Schizoid

. . . all of which are Personality
Disorders. See, I've learned a lot from

Sandy,
Hello ! ! RAD has damaged ALL OF me
and it has invaded all of me = all of
my personality . . . so it WOULD be a
PERSONALITY DISORDER . . . FOR SURE
. . .
And this is not an "excuse" for my
behaviors and actions now. That's the
unfair in all of this.

I was "set up" so to speak to be this
way . . .

> and yet I must bear full
> responsibility of my actions anyway.

> It couldn't work any other way
> anyway.

> > I "pay" for what I "do."
> > Regardless of what kind of
> > hand my parents dealt me.

> > I'm still responsible for how
> > I play those cards TODAY.

* Seems like I've written so little on the
healing part of the journey. It's because
the healing journey – while it has some
common elements to it – is so different
and varied for each person.

A piece of the healing journey for the "WHY?" questions to finally – they need to be asked but probably will not all be answered – morph into "WHO?" or "WHAT?" questions.

WHOSE fault is/was it, really?
WHO is God, really?
WHO am I, really?
So now, WHAT do I need to do to heal?"
    WHAT do I want?
    WHAT do I need to move forward?
    WHAT do I do with all of this
        "baggage" (past stuff)?

The only REAL answer to the "Why me?" question is . . .

"I DON'T KNOW."

Followed by . . .

"What I DO KNOW NOW is . . .

    It's *not* my fault
    It's *not* because I'm bad or not
        lovable
    It's *not* because God doesn't care . . ."

"Yes, bad things happen to good people . . .

    "but, why me?"

"I DON'T KNOW."

Letting go of the "why?" is REALLY hard to do . . .

> Because I WANT TO MAKE SENSE of it all
> Because if I can make sense of it . . . then I know what to do/not do NEXT TIME so it won't happen again

(CONTROL).

> BUT . . . if I CAN'T make sense of it/figure out the "Why," then I WON'T know what to do/not do next time

(OUT OF CONTROL).

> > PLUS . . . my brain wants to understand . . .

But . . . how can a brain make sense out of something that's "sense-less?"

It can't.

Because it truly is SENSE – LESS.
It is void of anything that can make sense in the first place.

And nobody will even be able to make SENSE out of something that is truly SENSE – LESS.

So . . . the best answer to "Why?" is

I DON'T KNOW. But here's what I DO know,

* Here are a few of the healthy cognitive thoughts . . . the "Both – And" thinking: "I CAN BE SAFE . . . EVEN IF . . . (both-and) =

I don't have all the answers
I don't have all the control
I don't have all the choices
Someone touches me
I'm not in "charge" (control)
I make an honest mistake
I don't know the future
I'm around other people
I can't "fix" it RIGHT NOW !

It waits until tomorrow
Somebody disagrees with me
I disagree with somebody else
I didn't double check all the locks
I forgot something.

More like "EVEN WHEN . . ."

* I told Sandy today in our session,
which went well by the way, that (I think)
before healing/change can begin to
happen, several things have to be "in
place" first:

(1) old tactics aren't working well
anymore
(2) the cost of the old tactics is "too
costly" - now. The cost is
outweighing the "benefits"
(3) there is enough "ego strength" to
be able to deal with all the "stuff"
inside
(4) External environment is:
    (A) safe enough now (in
        actuality)
    (B) supportive enough now to
        open "Pandora's Box"
(5) there's at least 1 person (human
being) with which to interact - even
if that's a therapist.

She agreed.

* The TRUTH/REALITY is a key issue here. With a HUMAN BEING to speak / reflect / live that truth out and reflect it back to me.

   Because my perception of reality IS skewed and my beliefs are NOT true.

* There's a HUGE sense of LOSS somewhere along the healing journey where you find out just exactly how much of LIFE/LIVING you LOST to the survival mode of the jungle war . . .

   AND the RAD / survival mode you KEPT using ("jungle war in the soldier") . . .

That's a WHOLE LOT OF LIFE LOST . . .

   that can never be regained . . .

      just BEGINNING living from this point on is all you can do.

But what's been LOST . . .
                    is LOST . . .
                          FOREVER . . .

AND that's a WHOLE LOT OF GRIEVING.
And it will take time. As the "adult," I
can understand/see just how much has
been LOST. I can comprehend that.
It's DO-ABLE it just HURTS.

(And I have to remember it's "PAIN
#1" . . . only.)

* Slowing/changing the ANXIETY
thinking of "What if . . . what if . . . what
if . . . lions, tigers and bears . . . oh my!"
is a HUGE piece of the healing and the
"SAFE" process. I like the "3 x 5 + 1"
technique[13] Sandy suggested I "just try."

(1) Name 5 colors I see
(2) Name 5 sounds I hear
(3) Name 5 things I physically feel
(4) "What do I need to be thinking
about/doing RIGHT NOW?"

Training the brain to stay in the
present MOMENT is a BIG – and HARD
– task. But do-able . . . and NECESSARY
for health and freedom.

Likewise changing the
PERFECTIONISTIC thinking from
"should-shouldnt" to "could-I wish-I
choose"[14] is HUGE (another "just try it"

suggestion from her). This connects to the "tactics" used to keep safe. A HUGE list of "should do" and "shouldn't do" behaviors and actions.
Exchanging "should / shouldn't" for . . .

"Could"
"I wish"
"I choose" . . . IS REALITY . . .
it is the TRUTH.

HARD to change . . .

Because the "should" sounds so . . . good . . . true . . . accurate . . .

And I do want a guarantee that if I do the "right thing" then I won't get hurt . . . at all.

With the "could" . . .

BAD things COULD still happen to me!

NO . . .

NOT acceptable at all!

RUN.

But it's true . . . there is no "guarantee"
- not really this side of heaven. As much
as I want one.

So how can I still be "SAFE" without a
guarantee?

. . . in the
moment.

* There's the "damage" RAD does to a
person and then there's the
"collateral damage" that is as a result of
living with RAD's presence. For
example, FRIENDSHIPS in the later years
of life. The "friendships" that are deep
and well established for "elderly" people
were formed during the younger years

Because of a common bond through:

college years
military experience
fraternities or other "club"
association
job setting
growing up in the same
neighborhood
some "common bond" that began

in the younger years and has been fostered throughout the following years.

The friendships developed and cultivated during these years (20s – 50s+) are what will "endure" into the "elderly" years of the 60s and beyond. Fewer "new" (deep) relationships develop after that. And the ones that do develop happen between 2 people who: (1) know how to trust and (2) have many decades of socialization under their belt.

NOW ENTER RAD . . .
    Where other people are seen as:
        Competition
        The enemy – "foe"
        "Sources" to get from

    And there is no "time" – or reasons – for "friendships."

The RAD person, when they hit their 60s or beyond – assuming they've even healed from the RAD – STILL get slammed with being:

(1) alone
(2) not fitting in
(3) not belonging

(4) often divorced, not married
(5) with little or no experience in "socialization" skills

These all but condemn us to a CONTINUED life of solitude and aloneness.

Besides most healthy people in their 60s + have their friendship groups formed and "tight" with not much time, or patience, for a "new-bee" who's still learning the Junior High social stuff.

So even when you get the jungle war out of the soldier, it still is there to a certain extent. And it still is present enough to continue to torment long after the fatigues have been put to rest.

The best chance, really, for an aging RAD adult is to still be in a marriage that's survived all the flak RAD dished out on both parties. Then there's at least 1 person where a "friendship" can possibly be grown. The reason I say "possibly" is it depends on how much shrapnel damage the RAD has inflicted on the mate.

My marriage was destroyed by ME living out the RAD stuff. I have to take the blame for that outright. At least my ex- is still on talking terms with me and we seem to get along. I've finally started sharing some of this stuff I'm learning and trying to do and she seems genuinely interested and caring. I've never had a "friend" before but from what I can imagine, this is at least close. Don't know. It's still all new to me.

ANYTHING and EVERYTHING is a danger just waiting to explode on ME!

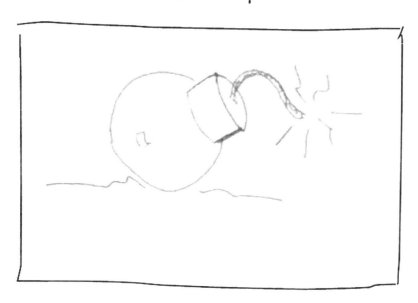

tick . . . tick . . . tick . . . tick . . .

* Another "ALL or NOTHING" form of thinking:

NORMAL   RAD

continuum of "possible"

1. not possible   1. not possible
2. possible   (NOTHING)
3. probable
4. likely
5. highly likely
6. almost certain
7. for sure / certain

2. FOR SURE . . .
   If it's "possible"
then
   It IS a "real"
danger!
   (ALL)

The "NORMAL" continuum of 7 "possible" categories/options is TOO MUCH to go through in 0.0002 seconds (survival mode) and too complicated to sort out. The . . .

ALL	or	Nothing
Friend	or	Foe
Black	or	White

Polarization makes it do-able with the time allotted in RAD thinking.

It "just has to be that way."

What's ALSO LOST are the chances to LEARN how to differentiate between which is which and to accurately assess the situation for the accurate response.

* So . . . once RAD is being addressed and healed . . . there's a VOID IN THE LEARNING of how to accurately access situations.

"I JUST DON'T KNOW" is a common reality.

And the way I DO learn is experientially (by living it out) not by being told about it.

* Trial and error learning . . . I hate that!

Freud was correct about 1 thing "Not all is as it seems." It's true with RAD — especially the "FLIGHT" type of RAD survivors.

* A specific example of the "old RAD" polarized thinking that needs to be

changed/healed into "new accurate" thinking is this:

RAD – "If 12 good things and 1 bad thing happen in the same day, the WHOLE day is ruined."

> Because the day was <u>either</u> ALL good or it was ALL bad.

>> Additionally, it's likely the only thing logged in the memory bank for that day was the 1 bad thing. The 12 good things will likely be "overlooked" and not recorded.

So, when I look "back" on the day . . . what I "see"/remember . . . is the BAD and the whole day was a "BAD DAY."

> Healthy thinking – "If 12 good things and 1 bad thing happen in the same day, the day was good over all with the exception of 1 bad thing that happened."

> It was BOTH . . . 12 good things . . .

>> AND . . .

1 bad thing. And the good far outweighed the bad today.

And . . . it's OK – and IMPORTANT – to remember and RECORD the 12 good things that happened too.

That's just one example of the type of cognitive changes that need to happen during the healing process. It's do-able, but not always easy.

* I'm noticing that some of my "quirk-ie" behaviors have not changed or stopped . . .

BUT . . . the reason / motive / purpose for them HAS changed.

Before the "motive" was the old "DO it or you'll DIE!"

Now . . . it's merely a HABIT that isn't "bad" – and I'm not "bad" if I do it – and it isn't worth the effort to try to brake the habit . . . and since it's not a "bad habit" – there's no real reason it "has" to be changed.

What use to be a "survival tactic" is now just a "quirk."

Like wanting my back to the wall in a restaurant. It used to be so somebody wouldn't sneak up behind me and strangle me. Now it's "just because." No real "reason" anymore . . . "just because" . . . a "quirk" is all.

And . . . I don't go nuts-o if I must sit with my back to the room. It's not my preference, but "it's OK."

* I'm feeling more and more that my old "tactics" are turning over into "benign quirks" or habits. That can make life a lot easier.

* The lack of "object permanence" in a RAD person has many facets. One being that:

QUIET/SILENCE =
   "NOT GOOD ENOUGH" =
      WRONG =
                     HURT

The need for constant (or a high regularity of) affirmation (feedback) is needed and when things go "silent" for a bit ... that equals "not good enough."

* The famous: "If a tree falls in the forest and there's no one to hear it fall, did it make a sound?" philosophical question.

In psychological terms to a child the answer is NO.
No response from the parent / caregiver / anybody = "I don't exist."

"If I walk into the study and Father doesn't respond in any way (which was the case most of the time I entered Father's study), did I really enter . . . and do I really exist?"

   "NO."

Why do you think children - and teens sometimes - act out? That way they at least get some RESPONSE out of the parent. And even a negative response "Get out of here, can't you see I'm studying?!" is better than no response.

With no "object permanence" if I can't touch it, hear it, see it, smell it, taste it . . . it doesn't exist.

* That's why RAD kids hoard food in their mattresses when there's "plenty" of

food in the kitchen. Because I have to be able to roll over and see and/or *touch* it to know "I have food."
That's why RAD kids can be "too touchy" with a parent . . . because they have to be in *physical contact* with you to make sure you are "still there."

That's why RAD kids will call out to a parent for no real reason, just to be able to hear you and know you're still there.

Because if you're out of sight and out of hearing . . . you don't exist. Until I can see or hear you again. And during that in-between time . . . you left me . . . again. That's how I understand it.

That's why making plans, carrying out plans, and such are hard for a RAD person to do, because those are "abstract" and "not real" things you're asking me to do - like planning ahead to get my homework or a project done.

This goes back to a diminished or no Cause and Effect thinking.

This same lack of "object permanence" often gets carried over to the relationship with God - who I really

CAN'T see or touch or hear.

QUIET/SILENCE = "NOT GOOD ENOUGH"

= "God's upset with me." Or "God is punishing me."

And it's not that I don't want God to be close or real . . . I don't know how to understand *Him* unless *He is that real* . . .

Part of SAFE is:

QUIET / SILENCE = OK / still SAFE.

* I went back over my notes from "Saving Your Brain"[15] . . . and it's a sobering reminder of the damage . . . not just emotionally . . . the environment that produces RAD does to the brain too. It's not just "all in my head" like some people think. There's a "real" neurological element to it too.

It's not a PART of the healing journey but a RESULT of it that I can focus (attention wise) on <u>others</u> as well as <u>myself</u> now.

It's not that I didn't want to before . . .

I just didn't have the "resources" / time / energy (or so it seemed) to "look out" for anyone else but me.

NOW that I'm not in the jungle war and the jungle war isn't inside of me . . . AND life has "slowed" to a more "normal" pace:

(1) I have TIME to look around and notice – be kind to – others

(2) I have ENERGY / RESOURCES to share (now) with others

(3) It's SAFE ENOUGH (now) to let my heart come out of that box so that my "true colors" of compassion / caring / etc. can come out – now – finally.

AUGGG!

I HATE this RAD stuff . . . it NEVER seems to end . . .

really . . .

* The INTENSITY never goes away . . . it just gets MORE MANAGABLE is all.

I guess that's not entirely true, SOME of the intensity goes away and the rest becomes more manageable.

* It's STILL not fair!

* I guess what I'm trying to say is that it's still "close enough" inside that I can connect with it in a deep way very easily and I have to guard myself because I can begin to feel all the old all over again.

* Some level of it will probably always be here and will always need to be "managed" . . . which means there will always be some energy expended in "managing it." Bummer . . . but it's better – *much better* – then it use to be.

* My (maybe not for everyone) "cycle" of coping =

> (1) touch it – deal with it, talk about RAD or PTSD and share my story. Write it down.
> (2) get overwhelmed by it all – the "too much."
> (3) headache / migraine / feel sick
> Forget things
> Tried all the time

Doing the "hiding" routine
(4) go to SLEEP (that's a huge "hiding" technique)
(5) end up "foggy brained" for 2-3 days
"Hung-over" feeling
Fuzzy or buzzing in the head
(6) reconnect with the world
"Pull out of it"

UNTIL NEXT TIME

I TOUCH IT SOMEHOW . . . and it starts all over again with (1).

I can see the pattern in me clearly now. That's what it is and it takes about a week to go through all the "recovery" steps of the cycle. Then I'm OK again . . . for a while . . . UNTIL NEXT TIME either I go back to journaling/researching or something triggers my stuff.

* OK, here's part of why "life is so hard" (I find myself thinking and saying that a whole lot) for a RAD person. Follow this:

(1) "Normal person" does task "A" (whatever that may be) and it takes 50 units of ENERGY/EFFORT (whatever "50 units" would equate to)

. . .

(2) RAD person does same task "A" . . . but it takes 80 units of ENERGY/ EFFORT to do the same exact task

. . .

because . . . RAD person has to do:

50	units task "A"
10	manage/compensate for RAD
10	keep safe from becoming overwhelmed
+	
10	just trying to live as "normal" as possible

_____

80 units   JUST TO DO THE
           SAME THING . . .

And this is true even if task "A" is a fun and enjoyable task, it STILL takes more . . .

Which means – even for the healed RAD person – I'm running much CLOSER to my "TOO MUCH" level than a "normal" person is to theirs.

So . . . I'm MORE likely to be pushed into the "TOO MUCH" zone and get overwhelmed . . . or depressed.

And . . . when I do end up getting pushed into the "TOO MUCH" zone . . . I tend to OVER-REACT so that it takes even MORE energy/effort – and even LONGER – to get "back in balance."

NOT FAIR.

I HATE THIS STUFF!

THAT'S WHY . . .

    "Life is HARD!"
    "Life sucks . . . then you die."
    I want to AVOID
    I'm GUARDED (defensive) . . .

    because it's still here . . .

'til I die . . .

(and that's not soon enough. Even though I AM enjoying life now – it's still hard ! ! ! !)

IT'S NOT FAIR

          NOT AT ALL ... EVER

But what else can I do but keep living a:
                    healthy
                    managed
                    compensated
                    "accurate"
        thinking a life as is possible.

So: (A) deal with the rage/anger
          deal with the depression
          deal with the anxious
              thinking patterns
          deal with the loss/grief/pain
    (B) manage and compensate as best
        I can
    (C) enjoy the good things in life
        along the way – because there

ARE GOOD THINGS

Ecc. 12:12b-13

> "Of making many books there is no
> end, and much study wearies the
> body. Now all has been heard; here
> is the conclusion of the matter: Fear
> God and keep his commandments,
> for this is the whole duty of man."[16]

Life is hard, so enjoy things along the
way as best you can.

That's it . . . that seems to summarize RAD in it's HEALED form as best I can state it.

* And I AM learning to enjoy good things along the way because there are LOTS of good things along the way. There really are.

It's **BOTH . . . AND**

"Life is hard"

AND

"Enjoy all the good things around me as best I can along this journey of life."

* Just realized that in writing all this . . . there will be no ENDING to it . . . because the only time RAD "ends" is with a casket and a gravestone. I will never be "100% as if it never happened" until heaven.

I can only guess it's like any combat soldier regardless of which theater he served in; the outside war is over, he can be a civilian again, BUT . . . the war has changed him inside <u>forever</u> in many different ways (many, if not most, are NOT "see-able" by others around him). He's not the "same" man he was when he went off to war. And he doesn't want pity, just somebody to come along and acknowledge that it's OK.

Again, never being a soldier maybe I have it all wrong. I don't want to sound arrogant or minimize what real combat veterans have gone though. I'm just guessing what this RAD stuff would equate closely to, and that's my best guess.

So I . . . along with all the combat vets over the decades . . . adjust to "normal" life as best I can. I enjoy what I can, manage the impact inside of me (silently usually) AND live until it's my time to go home.

But here's the gig. A combat vet (assuming a "normal" childhood) has a "life" to come back to. He knows the social how-to stuff, he knows how to trust. He'd coming back to normal.

But for RAD it's not coming back to

anything. It's coming to for the first time, with none of the knowing . . . GRRRRRRRRRR . . .

* I am proud of our military. I'm a "military brat." I know the sacrifices that are made. I don't want to take anything away from what combat vets have to adjust to when coming "home" . . . I don't. Still . . . they're coming *home*.

They have a home to come back to. That's where a huge difference is. RAD is not *coming home* because there was never a *home* to come back to.

Anyway . . .

* This "healing" – like RAD itself – is on a continuum:

none - - - a bit - - - some - - - a lot
- - - most - - - all

Like the physical rehab on my hand idea. You work to get as much of the usability and range of motion back as is possible . . . whatever that amount is . . .

50 - 65 - 80 - 100%

And just because the patient (who did the BEST they could) was only able to regain 75% back doesn't mean they were lazy or gave up or didn't try or are just playing the "victim."

DAMN IT! I <u>DID</u> give it my best . . . I <u>DID</u> work hard . . . I DID deal with the pain of the "rehab" (which can be as painful as the pain from the original injury was). And this IS the best it's gonna get – this side of heaven.

So . . . when somebody – even a trained therapist – says "it's all 'fixable' . . . if you just try hard enough." Or "If you just make the choice to get better" . . .

YOU SLAP ME IN THE FACE ! You DON'T get it!

And don't do the "God" thing by telling me "With God, everything is completely healable, every time." Look around at all the UN-HEALED (i.e. "all better – without any blemish") people in churches who have prayed for physical healing.

The TOTAL healing WILL COME . . .

But maybe NOT this side of heaven.

Until then – when perfect healing is accomplished.

BELIEVE ME

> More than the theories
> More than your ideals
> More than your illusions
> More than your wishes . . .

BELIEVE ME . . . because I'm the one living it – experiential knowledge . . .

BELIEVE the real person over your good intensions.

I can say with confidence that the "healed" life I have now IS FAR BETTER than what I had before . . .

> NO, it's not "complete"
> YES, RAD is still here some

YES, it's MUCH BETTER than I've ever lived before.

And I am VERY, VERY, VERY GRATEFUL for what I have . . . and that I found a therapist who understood this stuff enough to be able to heal . . . and was willing to help.

It's not "complete" or "total" healing (the 100% thing) . . . but . . . MUCH better. And yes, it was worth all the PAIN and EFFORT it took to get this far. I remember not being able to say that for a long time because I didn't think it was worth it . . . Now . . . with enough years passed and the healing sinking in more and more, I can say that – with confidence –

"It was worth all the PAIN
BLOOD
SWEET
TEARS
TERROR . . .

It was WORTH all that to get to where I am today – and for me . . . it's the "75% usage" place.

So . . . APPRECIATE my "this far."

RESPECT my blood, sweat, tears and efforts (that you'll probably never understand – and that's OK)

THIS FAR IS VICTORY

I don't want or need your pity
. . . no way . . . I just don't want you
laughing at my limp when I walk through
the rest of my
                              life!

NO, it's not that I want you not to laugh
at me . . .

I JUST WANT YOU TO LEAVE ME ALONE . . .

BECAUSE I AM DOING THE BEST I CAN !

(And don't try telling me "if you only try
harder.")

* OK . . . slow down (me, that is). This is
not the jungle and it's not war anymore
so . . . (and whomever I'm "talking to")
is not the enemy.

   . . . Let me rephrase this . . .

      PLEASE . . . believe me . . .

         and

      PLEASE let me limp off in PEACE -
      because this is the first time I've
      been able to be "at peace" and it
      feels good.

so

PLEASE leave me alone and let me enjoy the rest of my years . . .

PLEASE just let me be and not tell me what "else" I need to be doing or how I need to be "growing" or . . .

and

(Please . . . don't "poke the sleeping bear!")

* Remember, RAD is on a continuum from:

All of what's been written is coming from the INSIDE of a RAD person who is on the lower end of the continuum – where

I marked it with a " ^ ".

If THIS MUCH DAMAGE has been done with "mild to moderate"

environmental trauma . . . imagine HOW MUCH MORE DAMAGE is caused to those who are on the more "extreme" end of that spectrum . . . and what they have to face!

* Imagine a child who's been orphaned in a country that does NOT value human life – especially the lives of little children, where there isn't much food for the getting and where children are "free targets" for whatever the society wants to do with them.
Or a little girl who's been through the foster care system because her mother was a drug addict and ends up getting sexually molested by a number of foster care "fathers."

I imagine a kid living on the streets where everybody IS out to get you or whatever you have, where the weather is your enemy, the police are your enemy, perps and winos are your enemy, even other kids are your enemies to some degree. And they've survived for any number of years.

And you take any of these kids and place them in a "nice loving environment with parents who care and love them" . . .

and you think they're going to . . .

> Do what? Respond with love
> and appreciation for "saving"
> them?

> That they will just start trusting
> you, magically some how b/c
> you "love" on them and provide
> "structure" for them?

There's too much damage to do that.

IT IS NOT FAIR!!

To me, to the people who had to live
and put up with me. It's not fair to all
the RAD kids/people who had it harder
– more traumatic – than I did (and I
didn't have all that much really).

It's not fair that in almost every country
on this planet you need a license to
operate an automobile on the highway . . .

but ANYBODY can have a baby . . . and then – for whatever reasons – end up treating it this way, whether that's on purpose or because the parent truly was "doing the best they could" . . . which still wasn't enough for the child. And they can get away with it.

I can feel the anger inside me. Against my parents and ALL the parents of this world who would DARE treat a child in such a way as to cause RAD in them.

IT IS NOT RIGHT!

It just isn't.

* So, what do I do now? I don't know . . .

The old MO "don't die." Is gone
(which is good)

But

There's no new MO yet.
   No new reason for
   living
      +
I'm still tired from
the decades of
"running"/"fighting"
      +
I REALLY enjoy
REST/PEACE/QUIET
finally
      =
_____
I DON'T FEEL LIKE
WANTING TO GO ON -
JUST LET IT STOP.

In this game of life called "Tag" . . . I FINALLY found "home base" . . .

AND NOW ALL I WANT IS FOR THE GAME TO BE OVER !

PLEASE LET IT BE OVER ! !

– So I can FOREVER rest, relax, and enjoy the calm I finally found.

PLEASE?

Please

please

* So what do I do now? I don't want to do anything now.

But it's not going to stop. The game isn't over yet . . .

So I KEEP ON KEEPING ON . . .

That can feel soooo much like all my years in the jungle war . . .

" . . . keep on keeping on . . ."

303

But it is better . . . and it is still the same (in some ways) too.

"Keep on keeping on" feels like suffering and it doesn't matter that I don't <u>want</u> to suffer any more . . .

    I guess "better life" would be described as:

        CHRONIC SUFFERING (still) . . .

        WITH . . . peace, calm and good things sprinkled in and along the way . . . and waiting to go home (die).

Don't get me wrong, I <u>DO</u> enjoy the peace / calm / quiet.

I AM VERY THANKFUL that the war inside is finally over . . . but I was just hoping that when the war ended . . . all the suffering would too. Some of it has . . . some of it's still - maybe always - here.

Oh well . . .

I will take - and be thankful for - "better" . . .

(but I don't want to
suffer anymore . . .)

* Back to the "I don't know."

Back to the "It's not fair."

There's one more thing that is NOT
FAIR: (maybe more . . .)

It's not *fair* that I do have a good
and wonderful life now.

That's *not fair* either . . . because
there are many who were "born in the
jungle war"
. . . survived the jungle and NEVER
made it out . . . NEVER . . .

And there's many who are STILL IN
the jungle war - or at least it's STILL
living in them.

Why me? . . .

Lucky?
Fate?
"God"?
Karma?
"Better fighter"? (NOT this
one) . . .

"But for the grace of God . . ."

(and the willingness of a good therapist.)

That's the only answer I can come up with.

Formula:

$$\begin{array}{r} 1 \text{ "not fair it happened to me"} \\ + \quad 1 \text{ "not fair it's so good now"} \\ \hline 1 \text{ VERY thankful and grateful person} \end{array}$$

who would <u>not</u> wish to live it
again . . . but would <u>not</u> trade it
either . . .

* Sandy and I had our last official appointment today. I can still go back for a tune-up if I need to, but no more regular weekly apts. Don't have words

. . . .

. . . .

It was _____?_____ . . . weird, hard, sad, painful, satisfying . . . don't know the right word or words. It was a lot harder to say goodbye than I thought. I mean, she's just my therapist not my friend . . . . . .

Not true. While Sandy is not my social friend like we think of when we use the word friend, she is a professional friend. Actually, a better phrase would be a professional parent! Yeah, all the professional boundaries and stuff are there as well as a connection that's more. I mean, you can't go through the jungle with another person without having a special, unique connection because of the shared time, work, pain and effort. The experience together changes both persons and there is a "together" bond between them that isn't between any two other people.

Sandy *is* my therapist friend. There we go. She's BOTH . . . therapist and (professionally) my friend. WOW . . . I can feel her smirking like she does sometimes. I think I actually was able to "attach" to her in a limited way. Wow . . . Who would have thought. Hummmph . . . . .

. . .

I'm glad the "therapy" is over. I'm sad
the time with her is over. I'll miss her.
I am - however - glad for her! She can
finally get a rest and get the jungle
fungi cleaned off herself. She's got to be
tired. And I don't know how many RAD
clients she has. Hopefully not too many
. . . God bless you Sandy.

It's weird. Saying goodbye - as hard as
it was - doesn't feel like she
abandoned me or left me or dumped me.
It's OK. I'm OK. Just sad is all . . . AND
still SAFE as she taught me to think.

I can see how she's been preparing me
for this. Sorta feels like I'm a young
adult leaving the family nest. NOW
THAT'S weird. Well, no it isn't. It does
feel like I'm grown up (finally) and
ready to venture out on my own. I don't
know if that was part of her treatment
plan or not, but I'm glad it happened.
Very different. Not bad, just very
different . . . new . . . unfamiliar . . .
but not scary or threatening.
Just . . . weird . . .

You know what's weird. I'm not a "client" anymore. WOW . . . if that's not a different way of thinking! I'm just me . . . and it's OK. I'm me. That too feels different to say and really feel and believe.

I'M ME

I'll have to get use to that. And it's OK.

OK, so if I were to take these pages, make 10 photocopies of them and paste them all here . . . that's what I feel inside.

And there STILL wouldn't be enough accurate words to express what all I'm feeling . . . OR . . . my thankfulness to Sandy.

THANK

YOU

SANDY

thank you . . .

* There's been a 6 month gap since I last wrote in here and I still have to consciously fight the old RAD thinking and feeling sometimes.

IT' STILL HERE . . .

YES, less often = victory . . .

YES, less loud = victory . . .

YES, less powerful = victory . . .

But . . . it's not "gone all the way" – I'm beginning to think it will NEVER be "gone all the way" and will always be here to some extent . . .
the limp . . .
and getting this far IS victory!

* I really do miss my weekly sessions with Sandy. Sad it's over.

But, like they say "all good things must come to an end," and she surely was a good thing in my life.

BLESS YOU, SANDY. BLESS YOU.

And there's STILL that strong desire inside that's saying "leave me alone" . . . and . . . "accept my limp and be 'satisfied' with me."

* You wouldn't keep pushing a person paralyzed from the waist down to keep trying and trying and trying to walk on his own, would you? I hope not. You accept the "fact" that's he's in a wheelchair and you modify your expectations of him (at least I would hope you would) to fit the "facts" - no pity - just reality.

That's what I long for . . . BUT . . . there's nothing to "see" that's broken in me. No MRI, no X-Ray, no nothing to "show" or "prove" there's actually anything wrong with me. So the expectation of me stays the same as any "ambulatory" man on the streets.

I desperately want that acknowledgement . . . AND . . . at the same time I realize I won't ever get it. It's disappointing . . . "same ole . . . same ole."

! ! That would be obvious, don't you think?

* Another Side note: Serotonin and Dopamine (the chemical that regulates the wake/sleep cycle and sleep patterns) are also closely inter-related. So, if RAD is fighting depression = Serotonin levels are likely low = Dopamine levels are *also* low disturbing the sleep cycle.

Add that to RAD's already existing tendency for sleep problems and it makes sense . . .

RAD IS <u>NOT</u> "JUST PSYCHOLOGICAL" . . .

      IT'S ALSO <u>VERY MUCH</u>
            BIO-CHEMICAL AS WELL !
Grrrrrrrr . . .

* This journal has been going on for a long time – can't remember just how many months/years it's been since I started . . . oh well, 8 years ago, I think. WOW! The point is that while my "social" abilities/skills, etc. are still not much better and while my whole reluctance to trust/ability to trust is still lacking, the ONE THING that IS <u>very</u> different is that:

    I DON'T FEEL AFRAID ALL THE TIME
          ANYMORE ! ! !

Feeling "afraid" (anxious) is now the "exception" . . . NOT the "norm" anymore ! !

YEAH ! ! ! ! !

That is one HUGE thing I can say has changed . . .

I still don't want to be hurt (obviously) . . . but I don't live in constant fear that any little thing will happen to cause me to be hurt.

YEAH ! ! !

* "Secure rational attachment is the exception rather than the norm."[17]

* I've been wondering when I started writing all this because it doesn't seem I have a feel for the timeframe as I look back over these notes. I didn't date anything. Didn't number anything . . . didn't do any organizing of this stuff at all. Sort of like RAD itself. Hummmmmm. Interesting.

"The deepest expression of any emotion is silence." Let the silence speak and do your best to understand that you won't be truly able to understand it.

RAD breeds . . . RAD . . . breeds . . .
    RAD . . . breeds RAD . . .

* Been thinking on this earned – secure attachment and here's what makes sense to me:

    Natural – SECURE attachment is like a LAKE.

    Earned – SECURE attachment is like a RESERVOIR.

    It functions in much (mostly) the same way as a lake
    It looks a lot like a lake . . . but it was *purposefully* "created" in a non-natural place and way.
    It didn't just happen . . . it was MADE.

So, while looking like and functioning like a lake . . . it's not . . . quite . . . BUT it's still GOOD to have . . . useful . . . functional . . . and TONS better than nothing.

Sort of like an artificial limb – not the same as a natural bio-arm . . . but very good to have in place of the non-existent bio-arm.

Good? Yes. But not as good as natural 100% healing.

* RAD will always leave it's presence in the person . . . someway . . . someplace . . . somehow . . . even if others don't see the limp . . . it's still there.

The most noticeable "parts" of NORMAL living that will likely always be missing are in the area of socialization. Again, that's obvious it would be there.

So LET ME BE . . . Let me be as I am . . . as I can. I will never be a social-ite or socially graceful. So just let me be quiet, withdrawn and let me connect as I'm able to.

The RAD "neurological pathways" (or whatever they're called) will ALWAYS be in the brain . . .

> BUT . . . don't have to be the DEFAULT pathways anymore.

BUT . . . ARE always there and can be "fallen into" at any point in time and for any reason.

So . . . it takes CONSTANT focus and energy to use the new pathways and stay out of the RAD rut pathways.
And believe me . . . it does take energy.

It reminds me of that game from when I was a kid called Labyrinth where you guide the marble through a maze by tilting the playing surface, and you try to avoid holes along the way to get it all the way to the end.

That's what every day feels like – ESPECIALLY around people. You try to keep out of the "holes" (RAD thinking) and not get "lost" in the maze of social interacting . . . all at the same time.
It's HARD ! !

I never was good at Labyrinth!

* Came across this the other day and it makes sense that RAD people would have some/many of these cognitive distortions:

CHECKLIST OF
COGNITIVE DISTORTIONS[18]

1. **All-or-nothing thinking:** You look at things in absolute, black-or-white categories.

2. **Over generalization:** You view a negative event as a never-ending pattern of defeat.

3. **Mental filter:** You dwell on the negatives.

4. **Discounting the positives:** You insist that your accomplishments or positive qualities don't count.

5. **Jumping to conclusions:**
   (A) Mind-reading – you assume that people are reacting negatively to you when there's no definite evidence;
   (B) Fortune-telling – you arbitrarily predict that things will turn out badly.

6. **Magnification or minimization:** You blow things way out of proportion or you shrink their importance.

7. **Emotional responding:** You reason from how you feel" "I feel like an idiot, so I really must be one."

8. **"Should statements":** You criticize yourself or other(s) and "have to's."

9. Labeling: instead of saying "I made a mistake," you tell yourself, "I'm a jerk," or "a fool," or "a loser."

10. Personalization and blame: You blame yourself for something; you weren't entirely responsible for, or you blame other people for the problem.

* What I see in myself = 1, 4, 5, 6, 8, 9, 10. 7 out of 10 distortions is NOT healthy . . . normal thinking AT ALL.

#1 – Of COURSE it's "all or nothing." In survival mode it IS black or white . . . friend or foe . . . do or die. I've been saying this all this while.

#2 – I can see this because in RAD things are almost always viewed in the NEGATIVE rather than the POSITIVE. Daha !!

#3 – I can see this. "Lions . . . tigers . . . and bears . . . oh my!" will always see the NEGATIVE . . .

#4 – Daha ! !! Those "accomplishments" (that are in the past) will NOT do anything to keep me alive NOW. "Besides, it was luck anyway." And there's no time in war to glory in one's accomplishments anyway.

#5 - You HAVE TO BE 1 STEP AHEAD of everything and everyone. You HAVE TO "mind-read" if you expect to survive.

#6 Because it IS DO or Die . . . it is that BIG of a deal . . . . it's survival for goodness sakes!!! It only takes ONE MISTAKE . . . ONE TIME . . . and you're dead.

#7 - Don't understand this one . . .

#8 - That's obvious to me! This is a no brain-er. The "should" statements are part of the ROE to keep me from being hurt again. And since it IS a do or die world . . . it IS a "HAVE TO" world ! ! If you expect to not die.

#9 - Only jerks "do" stupid things in a survival world. Part of the self-contempt is to keep you on your toes as a soldier/ survivor . . . and besides . . . it's my fault anyway (control illusion) and besides . . . I'm NOT lovable anyway . . . so that makes ME the loser, jerk, un-lovable person.

#10 - Because it IS all my fault: (a) because it can't be the grown-up's fault and (b) if it's my fault . . . then it can be "fixed" (controlled) by me - and I HAVE to have the control (illusion) . . . and (c) in survival it's all about <u>me</u> not dying = VERY PERSONAL.

So . . . RAD will likely have LOTS of "cognitive distortions" - that all MAKE SENSE in the jungle however . . .

Again, it's nothing new just collecting more info that relates to RAD and trying to put the various puzzle pieces into place to help show RAD a bit better.

Seems to me that normal people -

RELATE

and RAD people

INTERACT

That connection between two people that is deeper than the topic / issue/ connect-task / etc.

That interchange of content / idea / but lacking that intangible component called "the connectedness" (for real).

Maybe it's a soul-to-soul connection that goes deeper into the person - not just deeper into the topic

Interactions can be:
Genuine
Meaningful
Caring
Respectful
Etc.

Don't know for sure so it doesn't mean it's fake to try to describe or pretend or manipulate.
It's just lacking the "_____" it . . . thing . . ."soul-to-soul" contact element.

Maybe I can't . . . b/c I'm RAD . . .

Webster's dictionary[19] time:

Attach – to fasten, to join, to connect by ties of affection.

Bond – anything that binds, fastens or unites, shackles.

Bind – to tie together, to hold or restrain, to fasten together.

Fasten – to attach: connect, to make secure.

Connect – to join two things together, to show or think as related.

Join – to bring or come together, connect; unite, to become a part or member of.

Together – in or into one group, place, etc., or in union, considered collectively.

Union – a grouping together, being united.

Unite – to put together as to make one; combine.

Interact – to act on one another

"inter" = between two or more people
"act" = movement/action.

* Yet another way/sequence to consider in the healing process:

(1) PAIN –
    (The old MO of "stop the pain now!")

(2) Realize the TWO KINDS OF PAIN –
    Awareness that "THIS" pain won't destroy . . .

(3) So . . . I am SAFE (really) . . . anyway . . .
    . . . even <u>in</u> THIS pain

(4) Which allows my brain to use the frontal cortex thinking for better decision-making

(5) Which . . . with better choices, will increase my chances of keeping myself SAFE and dealing effectively with the PAIN

(6) So I can get rid of THIS pain more quickly . . .
and in healthy ways

(7) Which makes me SAFER

(8) So I CAN relax . . . really (again/ more)

(9) Which allows my brain to think more clearly and effectively

(10) Which keeps me SAFER all around.

* RAD has a HUGE impact on the Limbic System part of the brain (the amygdala, hippocampus, etc.)

The hippocampus part regulates the sleep cycle

NO WONDER RAD messes with a person's sleeping and why so many RAD people I've come to know have sleep issues ! ! !

* Here's what it feels like "after the RAD" =

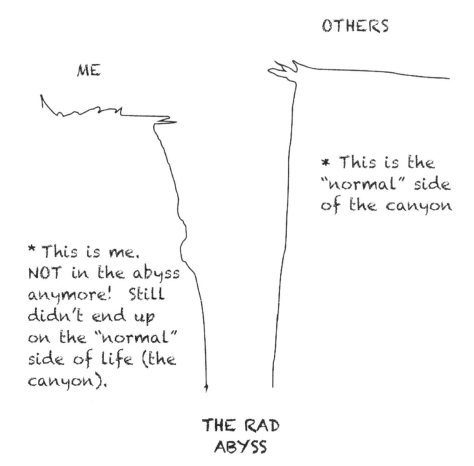

OTHERS

ME

* This is the "normal" side of the canyon

* This is me. NOT in the abyss anymore! Still didn't end up on the "normal" side of life (the canyon).

THE RAD ABYSS

VERY GLAD I'm out of the abyss ! ! ! ! YES ! ! !

Bummer this is where I ended up. But it's IMMENSELY BETTER than it was before. I'll take it!

* Even infants know when to stop crying . . . when it doesn't "work" anymore ! ! !

* When a pregnant mother has a high level of stress – high levels of cortisol in her system – this puts higher levels of cortisol in pre-born baby . . . and baby is BORN with a high cortisol level which is interpreted as "stressful" = "NOT SAFE ENVIRONMENT" . . . from the get go ! !

NOTE: STRESS in pregnant mother for any reason is still going to boost the cortisol level . . .

THEN . . . if mother STAYS stressed after giving birth (for whatever reason) it only "feeds" that cortisol into baby and keeps baby's already too high level of cortisol going and going and going and going . . .

And it was NOT baby's fault at all ! ! !

But baby is born an "adrenaline junkie." Which, I'm wondering, if that's any better than a FAS (fetal alcohol syndrome) baby. I would guess it has to be some better but . . . hummm.

* Respecting authority does NOT happen
– at least not very much or very easily
in a RAD person . . . because . . .

    (1) there are 2 kinds of "respect:"
        Earned
        Position/Rank (Father
            demanded respect-this
            one!)

A RAD person can develop a sense of
earned kind of respect because, "If you
treat me well" = you earn respect of
some sort. Of course . . . if you do NOT
"treat me well" you LOSE any and all
respect (all or nothing again).

    (2) since RAD is in a SURVIVAL
        mindset it's similar to the:

        "Abandon ship. Every man for
            himself!" situation.

            Which means . . .
            EVERYBODY
            is EQUAL . . . there is NO
            "rank" or authority
            structure left and it
            doesn't matter . . . ALL are
            equal . . . It's whoever gets
            the life vest first gets the
            life vest and whoever gets

into the boat first gets into the boat.

(3) So . . . there's no concept of RANK or POSITION (hierarchy) when all is "survive at all cost" or "last man standing" or "every man for himself."
There is no Admiral or Captain or Ensign it's only humans trying to "not die."

Wait a minute . . . this sounds familiar . . . the "abandon ship" thing, the "respect" thing . . . I remember writing this before. Hummmmm . . . Have to go back and look up where I wrote it.

And since RAD did have a "survival environment" – in which those who DID have actual RANK or POSITION (such as "mother" or "father" or "caregiver" or "God") did NOT PROTECT them or keep healthy order . . . there's an even greater contempt of RANK = because they failed me!

. . . and I got hurt b/c of it!

The very dynamic that started the RAD in the first place.

* I know all too well . . . "Son, you salute the rank not the person." . . . RAD people do NOT trust the RANK (position) OR the PERSON either . . .

Because BOTH FAILED ME ! ! !

* At least it's good to be where I am now! Amen to that.

* Thanks Sandy, for not giving up on me.

* Thanks God, for not giving up on me.

* So where do I go from here? I mean, this therapeutic journal is complete; it did its job to help me get here. I will keep it because it has a lot of ME in it.

I guess it's one day at a time like Sandy used to say. And today, IS a good . . . no . . . GREAT . . . day. Amen to that.

I guess too that I'll go back to my regular journal and let this specific one on my RAD journey close.

That sounds really good "my RAD journey closed . . ."

Amen to that!

AFTERWORD

This is a look inside the world of this vast subject called Reactive Attachment Disorder. The goal was to provide understanding and direction for those who are in a relationship with a RAD person and those who may have RAD. I also want you to know there is hope and there is a way out of the personal jungle a RAD person is in.

While there is no formula, no 1-2-3 step process to follow in the healing of RAD, there is a series of key elements to address. These are subject matters that have come up repeatedly in the years I've assisted RAD clients find their way out of their personal jungle.

Tom's journal follows a common progression from chaos to more organized and settled. There's a huge benefit to writing out your own narrative. Writing everything down helps you put the parts and pieces in the proper place and order. Getting things organized in your own written narrative assists in getting the past organized and settled in your mind and heart.

I.   AN OVERVIEW OF TRAUMA

The definition of trauma:

(1) Any serious injury (harm) to the body and/or mind, often resulting from violence or accident;
(2) Any event that causes great distress.

Distress:

> (1) Great pain, anxiety or sorrow
> (2) Acute physical or mental suffering, affliction or trouble
> (3) Exposure to pain

The ancient origin of the word trauma is from the Greek and it means to wound or damage.

> Trauma is caused when the body and/or mind is subjected to an impact (pain, anxiety, sorrow, etc.) that is greater than its ability to absorb (manage appropriately).

The concept of "managing appropriately" is critical because if the body/mind receives an impact and still maintains its homeostasis/balance we call it "unfortunate" but it's not traumatic. You managed appropriately the unfortunate situation. This is also known as resilience, the ability to flex, adjust and rebound from an unfortunate event.

Variables to Resiliency

There are many variables to resiliency. The presence of one or more of these variables can have direct impact on whether the event is experienced as a trauma or as an unfortunate event. Some variables to be aware of:

Physical age (especially if under the age of five)
Physical health, strength, conditioning
Mental health, stability, cognitive integrity,
     understanding
How traumatized the parents are/were (RAD breeds
     RAD breeds RAD)
Developmental stage of life
Spiritual stability, grounded-ness
Relational support system
Past trauma(s)

In summary, trauma is any exposure to an event which causes serious injury, great distress or damage. The person may: (1) experience the traumatic event directly; (2) witness the traumatic event in person; (3) hear that the traumatic event occurred to a close family member or close friend (often called secondary-trauma); or (4) experiences first-hand repeated or extreme exposure to aversive details of the traumatic event.

The notion that "what doesn't kill you makes you stronger" is not true. While trauma and hard times may build character in a person, it weakens the organic/biological brain. Trauma (and its aftermath—PTSD, depression, anxiety, and/or anger, etc.) destroys brain cells as noted by Jeff Victoroff, M.D. in Saving the Brain, Bantam Books, 2002.

Two Ways Trauma Can Occur

There are two different and opposite ways to cause deep wounded-ness or damage to a person.

The first—and most recognizable—way to damage another person is by abuse.

Abuse ("ab" = abnormal; "use"): Abnormal or inappropriate use of; words, physical contact, alcohol, sex, position of power, physical strength, etc.

Abuse is DOING something BAD to another person.

Abuse is what normally comes to mind first when we think of somebody being traumatized, wounded or is experiencing great distress.

The second—and less noticeable—way to damage another person is through neglect. It's less noticeable because it's hard to point to something that's absent or missing. How do you show another person a void? And because it's not nearly as noticeable or violent, people are far less likely to recognize or validate its existence. It may come as a surprise that neglect can be more damaging than abuse. Abuse says, "I notice you but I don't like you!" Through its silence, neglect says, "You don't even exist. You aren't even valuable enough to be noticed."

Neglect is NOT DOING something GOOD to the person who needs that good "something."

What Trauma Does to the Body and/or Mind

Think of the progression of trauma's impact in terms of the following diagram.

Pre-Trauma   Trauma   Post-Trauma

(Homeostasis)   (Deregulated)   (Attempt to regain homeostasis)

In the Pre-Trauma state, your body and mind are in a state of homeostasis or equilibrium. There is balance, order, sequence and organization present in both the body and the mind.

When trauma occurs the brain gets "scrambled" much like kicking an ant pile and watching the ants go everywhere all at the same time. We call that state of mind deregulation. The circumstances were beyond your ability to "manage appropriately."

Deregulation (the "scrambled-ness") can greatly thwart the brain's ability to think clearly, perceive accurately, judge wisely and make healthy decisions. This is especially true in children. The reason for this inability to think clearly is because the brain's locus of energy moves from the higher thinking portion of the brain (frontal cortex) to the amygdala (specifically the right-hemisphere) portion that regulates the survival "fight or flight" response. The amygdala doesn't think, it simply reacts/responds and is influenced more by sensation and emotion than data or language. It is primitive and simplistic in its evaluation of the present circumstance. This fight or flight state of mind can easily increase the chance of irrational behavior, anger outbursts, escaping behavior, etc.

Case Study

Say you are driving home after work. The radio is on and all is fine; Pre-Trauma.

Pre-Trauma

(Homeostasis)

Without warning you are in a serious crash. Trauma occurs, your brain gets "scrambled" (deregulated). You are subjected to an impact (pain, anxiety, sorrow, etc.) that is greater than your ability to absorb (manage appropriately). The severity of the accident is beyond your ability to maintain your Pre-trauma balance, order, sequence and organization in your body/mind and you lose your homeostasis.

Trauma

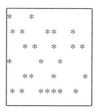

(Deregulated)

Everything stops spinning and comes to a halt.

You notice you are shaking and very sore but other than that you are not seriously injured. Both your mind and body go into "overdrive" as some say. You get the needed insurance and driver information. You recount the incident to the police officer. You gather your stuff together, pile into your friend's car (who came to your aid when you texted them) and have them drive you home.

The accident occurred, you got deregulated, you managed to "hold it together" and do what needed to be done. You get home and flop onto your sofa you begin shaking, crying and "falling apart". Why? The accident is over and everyone is alright (except your vehicle). Once you arrive at a safe place, all the "scrambled-ness" begins sorting itself out. This is the homeostasis place (Pre-Trauma state). You may experience any number of physical and/or emotional responses as you regain balance and sort through the trauma you just experienced.

Post-Trauma

```
*    * * * * *
* * * * *  *
* * *    * * *
* * * * * * *
     * *   * *
* * * *
```

(Attempt to regain homeostasis)

This re-balancing may take a few minutes, a few hours or several days. This is all the normal way the body/mind responds to a traumatic situation.

Case Study Summary

1. You were normal; Pre-Trauma.

2. You were Trauma-tized by the crash. You launched into survival mode and survived.

3. You got home and began processing all the various aspects of the crash and eventually regained homeostasis; Post-Trauma.

What often happens in the life of a RAD person is they go from one "car crash" experience to another to another to another and there is no "sofa time" to process the trauma that just occurred before being hit with another traumatic situation. This is that permanent state of shock and deregulation that grows the jungle inside the RAD person. This is why reactive-ness becomes mandatory because there is no time to "process" anything. There is no chance to find your way back to homeostasis, so there is no homeostasis (not even a comprehension of homeostasis) in the jungle.

II.   SPECIFIC NOTES ON CHILDREN AND TEENAGERS

Specific Notes on Children

If you're thinking of adopting or are in the process of adopting a young child, do a thorough study of Reactive Attachment Disorder and begin looking for a therapist in your area—or beyond if you need to—who specializes in this. You may never need to use their services and I hope you never do, but to have an understanding of what RAD is and how it can present is critical. To have a therapist already selected in advance "just in case" will save you time and heartache if the need ever arises.

If you have already adopted a child and things are going well, great, still research this topic. This is not to cause paranoia, but again, it's better to be aware, informed and prepared if things like this ever arise. I'm not saying that every adopted child will present with Reactive Attachment Disorder. While there is a higher likelihood of it, by no means is it true for every adopted child. Still, being aware is always wise. You get the idea; educate yourself and prepare yourself —always a sound principle.

If you have a child (any child) who is acting out and nothing seems to be working; consequences, rules, therapy, etc. research RAD and see if this might be what's pouring gasoline on the fire so to speak. A key principle in human behavior is this: we always do things for a reason(s) and if you can't seem to find the "reason" why your child is behaving the way they are and other avenues have already been checked out, at least consider (not assume) RAD and pursue it further. It may not be Reactive Attachment Disorder but if RAD is present and goes undetected, no amount of therapy, "tough love" or hugs will remedy the behavior. You'll end up wasting a lot of time, energy, sanity and money on things that won't work. At least look into the subject and remember, it's not limited to adopted children.

Specific Notes on Teenagers

If you're thinking of adopting or are in the process of adopting an adolescent, do the same thing I mentioned when adopting a child. Research Reactive Attachment Disorder and begin looking for a therapist in your area who specializes in this disorder in adolescents (which is less common than therapists who work with RAD in children). Hopefully you will never need to use their services, but again, to have one already picked out "just in case" will save you time and heart ache if the need ever arises.

Similarly, if your teenager is acting out and nothing seems to be working; consequences, rules, therapy, etc. research RAD and see if this might be what's pouring gasoline on their fire. There are plenty of rebellious teenagers that have no connection at all to RAD but if nothing seems to be working, it's worth checking RAD out. If RAD is not the underlying issue, that's good to know. If it seems like it might fit, then hunt until you find a therapist who understands RAD and works with adolescents to have it addressed.

A Second Chance

According to a study conducted by Judy Cassidy, there are two "natural" times in a person's life where a secure attachment can be made. The first being the first 12 months of a child's life. The second natural chance for making secure attachments is during the adolescent years when the youth is seeking out a mate and wants to be in a close, connected relationship with another person (as in a marriage).

Based upon how much damage was caused with the first failed attachment attempt the adolescent can be put in a difficult position to maneuver toward the second attachment attempt. My visual mind sees it this way; picture an aircraft carrier, if a person misses the landing deck of the "attachment" aircraft carrier in infancy they have one more "go around" to see if they can make a landing – a successful attachment.

However, since so much is going on during adolescence—physically, emotionally, socially and environmentally—the likelihood of making a secure attachment often goes by without notice or assistance. Additionally, the past trauma has made the adolescent defensive—and those defense mechanisms most likely are still "working" at this point—so that being able and willing to deal with the damage is often not an option. The brain won't let an adolescent open "Pandora's box" if there isn't enough ego strength, maturity and support to process what's inside. It's called survival.

This is why without intense and aggressive therapeutic intervention, I don't see a teenager being able to deal with all—at least not COMPLETELY—the RAD issues inside:

>   (1) Because their tactics are still working well enough; at least in their eyes;
>   (2) The "benefits" outweigh the "cost" for now;
>   (3) There is NOT enough "ego strength;"
>   (4) Sometimes their environment is still NOT safe enough or supportive enough.

Still, it doesn't mean you don't help a teenager. You work with all the issues listed on these pages and work through as many "layers of the onion" as they are able. Each layer you guide them through is going to help their life and the lives of those close to them. And yes, you may see there's more to do but they may not be able to get to those layers at this time. With each layer you do work through it will be that much less work to do in the future. And who knows . . . you may be able to get through all the layers of the onion because the RAD continuum is so broad, from a few to many layers.

III.   THE HEALING JOURNEY

A good all-around place to begin is to acquaint yourself with a number of topics that may be applicable to your particular situation. You don't need to be an expert in mental health disorders to have a good grasp on this subject matter. Make yourself aware of what may be present so if it is present you'll be more likely to pick up on it. A few topics to acquaint yourself with:

>   Adult Children of Alcoholics (ACOA)
>   Sensory Processing Issues
>   Anything you can find on "attachment pain"
>   Borderline Personality Disorder
>   Domestic Violence – Perpetrator or Victim
>   Narcissistic Personality Disorder
>   Adult Attachment Interview
>   Asperger's Syndrome Disorder
>   Schizoid Personality Disorder

If you are married to—or in a close relationship with— an adult who displays RAD thinking, seek help for yourself if necessary so you can keep your sanity and bearings. Their "not normal" thinking can cause you, over time, to doubt your own sound judgment.

If you are in a relationship with somebody who seems to present the particular profile of a domestic violence perpetrator, seek assistance as soon as you are able from a qualified professional or a community center that assists those in these kinds of situations. Don't wait and hope things will get better or that "it will all blow over." At least get the necessary information to help you better assess your present situation and make a list of things you can do.

If the person with RAD is open to addressing some of these issues, again, find a qualified therapist who understands RAD in adults. It will be a hunt, but it's worth the effort to find a person who professionally understands.

The two things you can't do are: (1) fix them and (2) fix it for them. RAD needs to do the work themselves to get healed. You can encourage, assist, cheerlead and listen. You can attend their therapy sessions with them if that helps. Be mindful to set—and keep—healthy personal boundaries so you don't get lost in their jungle. That's not to say you don't care about them. We just don't need two people trying to find their way through the jungle.

If that person with RAD is you, or you're wondering if it is because it seems to fit, there's help. Use this book to assist you in beginning your expedition out of your personal jungle. Find yourself a qualified professional who is a good fit for you. I will say on behalf of all the people whose stories have been compiled here, you're not alone even though it has felt like that your entire life. Find help. Yes, check them out carefully and keep looking until you can find somebody you can work with. You can find your way out of the RAD jungle. I know, I've watched, assisted and walked with a good number of RAD men and women, teens to 60 year olds, as they found their way to "Normaltown, USA." They did make the transition from "the jungle still inside the soldier" to the "civilian life." And maybe, just maybe, someday you'll be able to recognize the war is finally over.

On upcoming pages is a rough, (pencil-sketched outline on a paper napkin—you get the idea) of the common therapeutic goals I've identified over the years while working with RAD individuals. This is not a comprehensive treatment plan. Use this outline, adapt it, add to it, edit it, discuss it with your therapist; do whatever you need to do to assist yourself—or another person—to heal.

INSIDE: Understanding How Reactive Attachment Disorder Thinks and Feels

Outline for personal work

Note: Several goals referred to are familiar in mental health and are well documented. I defer to those materials and professionals who have expertise in that particular area of counseling. This sketched outline focuses on the points that may not be so familiar.

I use the analogy of how the medical profession deals with serious trauma and divide the healing process into four phases:

1. Get Out of the Line of Fire
2. Emergency Room Surgery
3. Recovery
4. Rehabilitation/Ongoing Life

While I address the phases separately, the RAD person may find himself or herself moving back and forth between phases any number of times. That's to be expected. Here we go.

1. Get Out of the Line of Fire

Before you can provide First Aid or any other kind of support, you must get the person/yourself out of the danger/threat zone. Soldiers, ambulance paramedics, law enforcement officers, firefighters and Search and Rescue team members know this. You may need to end an unhealthy relationship with a damaging person. You may need to change one or more community activities where the damaging people also attend.

It may mean physically relocating. It may mean getting help to stop addictive behaviors. You may have already done so, if you have—GOOD.

Getting children or adolescents out of the line of fire can be a difficult, legally tricky undertaking and will have its limits. Minors tend to get sent to therapy or a treatment center only to be returned to the active firefight in the home. Minimal healing work can be done until the immediate danger has been eliminated. If the person with RAD is still in an actively destructive environment (the RAD jungle), it's the RAD that's keeping them alive.

As much as you can, help the person by encouraging them to get out of the line of fire first. STOP THE TRAUMA.

What steps need to be taken to stop the trauma?

Create the plan!
    Action steps
    Contact information
    Permissions if needed
    Etc.

2. Emergency Room Surgery

The second triage point is to deal with the immediate trauma that is present. The healing journey for a RAD person is similar.

Answer the following questions in your journal:

What are the deepest wounds?
Do they/you have a SAFE place to live?
Where is the worst pain?
Are there any addictions that need to be confronted?

Do they/you have a stable job so the finances are SAFE enough?

Where is the bleeding?

What is the damage?

There are at least seven issues to address during this phase. This is where the most intense work will be accomplished:

1. Deal with acute PTSD that's present
2. Define SAFE accurately
3. Separate the Two Kinds of Pain
4. Look at the ROE (Rules of Engagement) and the "tactics" used to keep SAFE
5. Do a Lost List and grieve the losses
6. Address Cognitive Distortions that arise
7. Address Anger/Rage that may arise

Deal with Acute PTSD that's Present

In the Emergency Room, it's first things first. Deal with any PTSD that may be present.

P = Post, after the fact
T = Trauma that was experienced
S = The Trauma is causing Stress on the person
D = The Post Traumatic Stress is significant enough to cause Dis-order in the person's social interactions, capacity to work or other important areas of functioning.

Active triggering, nightmares, flashbacks, over-reactions to common events need to be eliminated or greatly diminished first. Even though the person is physically out of the line of fire, in a mental sense, the trauma is still active in the psychological sensations their body/mind is experiencing. You can take the soldier out of the jungle war, but it's harder to take jungle war out of the soldier.

I defer to the materials and professionals proficient in dealing with PTSD.

If there is no active PTSD at this time move on to SAFE.

Define SAFE Accurately

Safety is fundamental in Maslow's Hierarchy of Need pyramid and it's the center focus of RAD. SAFE, what it is, what it isn't and if it even exists must be addressed early in the therapeutic process.

How would you (not Webster's Dictionary) define the word SAFE? What would circumstances have to be like in order for you to feel SAFE? Do you think SAFE even exists? Take your time to work on a definition. Be careful not to make your definition what you think it should be. Being honest is critically important when it comes to being free.

Once you have a definition that seems agreeable to you, compare your definition with the dictionary's definition. Ask others how they would define the word SAFE. How does their definition compare with yours?

SAFE will always be important, even in "Normaltown, USA". Developing an accurate definition of SAFE is foundational to being able to feel the SAFE when it's present. A person can empirically/factually be SAFE—not in any danger whatsoever—

but not feel SAFE at all because of a default in their internal definition around what SAFE is or must be.

Early in the Tom's journal the word SAFE was defined as "Significantly Away From Everyone." Follow this line of thinking, if that is a person's working definition, where are they going to be able to find such a place on this planet—short of Northern Alaska somewhere? Most likely the answer is "nowhere". So if that's your working definition will you ever feel SAFE? No. Not because you are actually UN-SAFE, but because your definition isn't accurate enough to allow you to recognize and feel the SAFE you are standing in at that moment.

In comparison, look at the definition on page 234, where SAFE is redefined as "Solidly grounded, Assertive, Friendship, and Exercising healthy level of control." Is this definition of SAFE likely to be found somewhere in a person's experience? It is much more likely than with the first one. This accurate definition opens up the RAD person to feel the SAFE that is (empirically) already present. The felt safety is what our minds and bodies rely on throughout our everyday experiences.

SAFE may be a subject the RAD person comes back around to again and again during the healing process and even as they walk around in the "civilian" world. Realize it and fine-tune your definition as needed along the way.

Separate the Two Kinds of Pain

Children are unable to regulate themselves. They are unable to find, keep and return to a place of balance and homeostasis emotionally on their own. This stage is called Other-Regulation because the child depends on another person—primary caregiver, etc.—to do the regulating for them . . . and . . . teach them about regulation and how to do it themselves.

In the years from elementary school to early high school the individual can't Self-Regulate—yet—but doesn't need somebody to do it for them . . . they need somebody to come alongside and do it with them. This is called Co-Regulation. This is when a parent, teacher, coach, therapist, etc. guides and assists the child in getting back to balance or helps keep them from going off balance when something bad happens.

Self-Regulating is the final stage of regulation—you are able to keep, find and return to balance yourself—and doesn't become solid until the mid-teen years and older. Self-regulation is a key element in developing resilience that helps us manage appropriately unfortunate situations.

A major part of regulating is learning the difference between what I call the Two Kinds of Pain. In short they are:

1. Pain that hurts because it hurts (no "damage done");

2. Pain that hurts because there is damage being done.

Example: When a child receives their immunization shots at 18 months of age, all pain feels catastrophic like, "It's gonna kill me!" They have no understanding of pain that will hurt but go away soon and not leave a damaging result. It's the parent, the Other-Regulating person, who calms the child and brings the child back to balance/homeostasis. And by doing so teaches the child the difference between the pain of a syringe and the pain that goes along with a broken arm they experienced when they climbed over the porch railing and fell. The broken bone pain indicates there was damage done and damage continuing to be done as long as the child keeps playing with that broken arm. The adult (presumably) knows the difference and through tone of voice, reactions, encouragements and responses exhibits the type of pain the child is experiencing.

In the RAD world there was not enough Other-Regulation—or any regulation—being taught. The differing kinds of pain were never successfully separated which means, even as an adult, the RAD person often feels any pain and all pain as, "It's gonna kill me!"

What's paradoxical with physical pain is the RAD person often has a very high tolerance for physical pain to the point they may be numb to pain, not feel pain (or only when it becomes extreme) and/or is almost impervious to physical pain. In the RAD jungle there was no time to stop, take off your boots and mend the blisters. You do that and you'll get your head blown off—so says the thinking of jungle warfare. You learned to suffer and found ways to ignore the blisters. Clients have shared stories of going days with a broken hand before visiting the doctor, or walking on fractured feet they "fixed" the best they could on their own. Others have shared experiences of leaving the hospital the very same day they had major surgery and returned to work the next day because they needed to put food on the table for their family. Working a physically laborious job 10 hours a day while nursing pneumonia or other serious sickness are common stories told to me over the years. So you do what you have to do to keep going. "If I'm not dead, I'm OK and I keep going" is a repeated mantra. One client posed the question, "What else could I do but go on?" Exactly. Stories like these show the other side of not learning to separate the Two Kinds of Pain, in that all pain is ignored—even the destructive kind.

Emotional and/or relationship pain is where the Two Kinds of Pain are welded together into one ironclad unit. It's at the core of attachment, the relationship between them and others and where pain is often felt the deepest.

"If I dump you before you dump me, I'm not the one getting dumped (rejected, cast away . . . again), so it doesn't hurt (as much)" is the way many RAD people approach relationships.

It's the all-or-nothing thinking, "I will give you one chance and if you blow it, I won't have anything to do with you ever again" even if that "blown it" circumstance was because you said you'd call at 3:35pm but didn't call until 5:00pm. "You lied to me and you can't be trusted . . . EVER." The black-or-white thinking pattern of a RAD person finds its way into so many aspects of the thinking that impacts relationships.

Now as an adult, the RAD person has to learn the skill and art of regulating. This is best done with a qualified therapist, friend or spouse who will be the "other" person for the Other- and Co- Regulation phases. Where another person is not available or willing to do so, the RAD person repeats a skill they know so well = figuring things out for themselves.

As the therapist I'm often the "other" person. One exercise I do—formally and informally—is to go through a situation my client experienced that week. As the pain part comes into the discussion I ask two questions: (1) "What kind of pain did it feel like?" Most of the time the pain was experienced as, "It's gonna kill me!" pain. I validate that truth, because it did feel that way, no question about it. Then I ask (2) "As we look back at the situation now, what kind of pain was it really?" Over and over again we walk through circumstances and slowly separate the Two Kinds of Pain.

How to deal with pain in healthy ways also needs to be learned. The jungle way was "fight or flight" (or numb) and that one way was applied to most all painful experiences. Learning what pain is for real takes rewiring the brain and often the body too. Remember, when working with the subject of pain you're dealing with the mid-brain which doesn't think it just reacts, that part of the brain that functions instinctively not cognitively. Being able to separate the Two Kinds of Pain adds to the world of SAFE as the two principles validate one another.

Regulating always begins with Other-Regulating, followed by Co-Regulating and finally to Self-Regulating. Separating the Two Kinds of Pain is a part of learning how to Self-Regulate. For a good number of my clients the bewildering thought is "You mean, I can feel pain and still be SAFE at the same time?" This may be totally new thinking for a RAD person and is as difficult to comprehend as talking Portuguese to them.

It's worth mentioning that you have an adult learning the things a child was supposed to have learned. There's likely to be over-reactions and under-reactions to pain over and over again. Reactions that are acceptable in a child, but "funny" or "weird" or "foreign" to the people around when it's in an adult.

This can be very embarrassing and humiliating to the RAD adult. And this can be one more voice reinforcing the "I don't belong" and/or the shame that's already inside.

Look at the ROE (Rules of Engagement) and the "Tactics" Used to Keep SAFE

The human mind is designed to survive at all cost. In the RAD jungle there was no consistent SAFE. There was no trust in people and the environment was chaotic, neglectful and/or abusive.

To survive, the RAD mind—in the young child—learns ways to be safe—or less UN-SAFE—and not get hurt . . . or . . . at least get hurt less. These behaviors I call "tactics." Collectively, I metaphorically refer to them as the ROE (Rules of Engagement). It's the law that was written internally to follow the "not die!" MO. But how appropriately and accurately can a child with limited knowledge, maturity and resources compile a healthy ROE? They can't. Additionally, the ROE manual has no index, table of context, no "spell check," no categories and not even written with the same color writing utensil. For a RAD person, tactics were invented, pieced together or stumbled upon accidently on the spot in the heat of the moment—to "work" for that moment. Tactic number 314 "Control by yelling" is the opposite of tactic number 1297 which says, "Agree and don't say anything", but both are listed in the ROE as rules to never break or else you'll get hurt. Contradictions like this often exist and make the RAD person feel schizophrenic inside. The ROE manual is as chaotic as the jungle . . . night-time . . . raining . . . with a firefight going on. There is no order, no sanity, and no consistency.

It's this ROE manual that needs to be written down so the RAD person can know it, hear it, see it, touch it and evaluate it. Most, if not all, tactics will have one overarching purpose: "don't die!" and subsequently; "How do I get what I need right now?" and "How do I not get hurt?" Keep in mind both questions are answered from a child's vantage point (not an adult's), as well as answered to fit specifically into the jungle war zone—not a "normal" environment.

Here's the twist. The tactics worked. They worked well enough to survive. The RAD person managed to "not die!" Wounded yes, emotionally disfiguring maybe, but "not dead". They were true to the MO all those years. I tell my clients they deserve some equivalent form of a Medal of Honor or Silver Star because they—as a child—figured how to survive by themselves in that personal jungle and make it out alive. Smart kid! That's true.

But using those same tactics now as an adult in the civilian world don't work. People think you're crazy when you go to the store with your combat boots, flak jacket, helmet and rifle. You're on guard and ready for anything (bad of course) to happen. You plan for the worst just like you always do when you go anywhere. The RAD person is still living with the jungle war inside their mind and/or body as they stroll through the local shopping mall. RAD in turn thinks the "civilians" are the crazy ones because who in their right mind would go anywhere "unprepared" for the combat that is out there just waiting and lurking around the corner.

Yes, some of the tactics may work today and some may even be accurate for today's world. Most will be antiquated—like trying to fight with bows and arrows when the modern would uses lasers. Most, even the ones that "work", come with a price that's too high to keep paying—the collateral damage is too great to keep ignoring as the RAD person ages.

I have the person list the tactics they use/used in order to "not die!" while growing up—and maybe even today. Don't evaluate the list yet, simply write them down and organize them as much as possible—possibly for the first time ever. It may be worth it to review the journal entries where tactics were listed (pp 318-19).

Reviewing the definition of SAFE and the Two Kinds of Pain may also help. That's because the tactics written in the ROE manual were developed in conjunction with the whole reality of SAFE—or its absence—and which never had the opportunity to separate the Two Kinds of Pain. While SAFE, the Two Kinds of Pain and tactics are broken out separately, they are intricately interwoven in real life.

Then I have them compare their ROE list with what healthy people around them do. What tactics do they use to keep SAFE—in a healthy way? What tactics did you learn that are acceptable to keep because they are accurate and healthy? What tactics are "out of date" and not used by healthy grown-ups? What is the old tactic costing you every time it gets used? Is it worth the cost now that you're in the civilian world? You get the idea. Compare, contrast and rewrite your ROE to match the adult normal world you are in now. Old habits die hard.

Changing all these perceptions in your brain will take time and repetition. It will take time and repetition. It will take time and repetition.

The Lost List and Grieving the Losses

Another list. List all the things "lost" . . . or . . . you never had a chance to "get" in the first place. Include the tangible and intangible things that were lost or never received. When we talk about "loss" we think of a person dying and the grief that comes with that loss. This Lost List may include people close to you who have died or moved away and with whom you lost contact. It may be when parents divorced. These are the tangible things lost; a pet, a favorite toy or a treehouse to play in. The intangible things are many: loss of safety, loss of your childhood, loss of innocence, loss of a quiet environment to learn normal things, loss of any sense of worth or value, loss of calmness and stability, loss of nurturing, loss of enough validation and affirmation, etc., etc., etc. Think about things a child would usually receive growing up in a healthy environment. How many of those things did you not get or not get enough?

Once again, here is where another person can talk things over with you and help you compose such a list. I defer you to materials and professionals proficient in dealing with grief and loss process.

Address Cognitive Distortions That Arise

"You have your reality and I have mine" simply isn't true. Every human being is entitled to his or her own perceptions, attitudes, values, beliefs, and concept of the reality around them. What is real is still real. It was real before you were born and will still be real after you die. No human being owns reality. It isn't "my" reality. It isn't "your" reality either.

This is critical to understand when we talk about distortion. Distortion is a change in a person's perception so that their concept of whatever matter is at hand does not correspond with whatever matter is actually at hand.

I tell my clients sanity is when their perception of reality and reality match . . . in-sanity (unofficially) is when their perception of reality and reality don't match.

David D, Burns, MD in The Addictive Personality, put together a list of cognitive distortions that's frequently used in mental health settings:

1. All-or-nothing: You look at things in absolute, black-and-white categories.
2. Over generalization: You view a negative event as a never-ending pattern of defeat.
3. Mental filter: You dwell on the negative.
4. Discounting the positives: You insist that your accomplishments or positive qualities don't count.
5. Jumping to conclusions: (A) Mind-reading—you assume that people are reacting negatively to you when there's no definite evidence; (B) Fortune-telling—you arbitrarily predict that things will turn out badly.
6. Magnification or minimization: You blow things way out of proportion or you shrink their importance.
7. Emotional reasoning: You reason from how you feel: "I feel like an idiot, so I really must be one."
8. "Should statements": You criticize yourself or others with "have to's."
9. Labeling: Instead of saying "I made a mistake," you tell yourself, "I'm a Jerk", or "a fool", or "a loser".

10. Personalizing and blame: You blame yourself for something you weren't responsible for, or you blame other people for the problem.

NOTE: This same list appears on page 318-19.

How of many of these cognitive distortions did you come across in the journal? Again, I defer to materials and professionals proficient in cognitive behavioral therapy (CBT), of which there are many different forms.

Address Anger/Rage That May Arise

Anger/rage may or may not be present now/yet and I realize every person's journey is different. Still the emotion of unfocused rage is the one over-riding, intense, deep down in the depths of the soul emotion that comes with RAD. Anger is a combination of HURT plus WORRY and there are lots of both of these emotions everywhere you turn in the jungle war where the RAD person lived for all those years. Plus, children have an inborn natural instinct to react negatively to injustice. You add those two sources of anger into a child that believes all pain will kill them, placed in an environment where there is no one they can trust, and you get . . . RAGE. Lots of it.

Be aware too that in order to not get hurt (or not get hurt worse), the rage a child has often gets: (a) turned on themselves with self-harming behaviors, (b) locked inside which will ooze out in any number of physical ailments and/or (c) aimed at others who are less powerful and can't hurt them back. So, whether the RAD person is aware of it or not, be mindful and ready to address anger when it does surface.

With that said, I defer to materials and professionals proficient in dealing with rage and anger management. Let me add one thought; make sure the therapist is informed on reactionary responses, how the amygdala part of the brain operates and how to reprogram the auto-response system.

3. Recovery

All the work you've done to this point is what gets you off the operating table and into the Recovery phase. This is when you allow the wounds to mend, the changes to become established as the new normal. The goals to address now are:

1. Learn you HAVE TIME
2. There are some goals to continue working on
3. RECONNECT yourself—your mind, body and emotions
4. CHOOSING to make CONNECTIONS

HAVE TIME

The biggest thing to learn during recovery is that you HAVE TIME. There is time to heal. There is time to rest. There is time to fix that problem, tomorrow. There is a tomorrow. The "now-or-never" may still scream in your head (the old jungle thinking) but you do HAVE TIME . . . now.

Remind yourself—daily or even hourly—you do HAVE TIME. Review circumstances that proved you really did HAVE TIME . . . and . . . how the world didn't come to an end either. Be mindful how HAVING TIME and your definition of SAFE are intertwined. HAVING TIME is an important part of the definition of SAFE.

Keep Working

The second part of the recovery process is continuing to work on the changes made to this point:

> Your definition of SAFE
> Separating the Two Kinds of Pain
> Changing out your old "tactics" for modern ones
> for your ROE
> Listening and changing any COGNITIVE
> DISTORTIONS you may come across—
> still.

Reconnect Mind and Body

Almost every RAD person has some amount of "disconnected-ness" from their emotions and/or their physical body. Back to your definition of SAFE. It is SAFE now, to reconnect with your emotions and learn healthy ways to process and express them. It is SAFE now to reconnect with "that body" and learn healthy ways to keep it SAFE and care for it, because you do HAVE TIME now to care for "your" physical body. Getting a therapeutic massage, learning relaxation techniques, practicing deep breathing skills are just a few ways to connect your body and mind back together.

Choosing to Make a Human Connection

You may or may not be ready to address this yet. If not, that's okay, plan to loop back around later and face it. Begin CHOOSING to make CONNECTIONS with at least one other human being. Some need to begin by attaching to an animal first. That's fine. The goal however, is to connect with a human being. This is a risk, this is new, this is unknown and you may not be sure it's even necessary. Slowly search out a person who's healthy and trustable and see if you can begin to make a personal human connection with them. You may need an activity or interest as the focus point for the relationship. Most often this is the case for men. Again, here is where a qualified therapist can coach you along this journey. It may be that your therapist is the first attachment person. This relationship will be limited to professional interactions only, yet it can be a great starting point—a stepping-stone to personal attachment.

4. Rehabilitation/Integration into Life

You are finally discharged from the hospital so to speak. The majority—if not all—healing is completed. The focus now becomes looking forward and learning civilian skills you never got the chance to learn as a child.

"Will I ever be 'normal'?" you ask. Yes . . . and . . . no. You will never be the "as if it never happened" normal. The jungle was real, RAD did happen, and the damage was/is real. All that is a part of who you are, what you've experienced and made you who you are today. It can never un-happen.

The "yes" answer is because you can develop what is known as a "new normal". You can gain normalcy. You can function normally. You can live a healthy life. It's "new" because it was never here before. It's new and it's normal both . . . even though the RAD jungle will never not exist in your past.

There's a good chance this civilian lifestyle, may feel soooooo boring and slow. That's because peaceful living is slower and more boring compared to the pace of surviving in the RAD jungle war that's been raging inside for so many years. But RAD is not a "normal" pace, a normal anything. The readjustment blues will take a while mentally and physically. I have seen it take two years or longer for the person's physical body to get hormone, neuro-transmitter and stress chemicals to healthy levels appropriate for their age. It may also take you a while to understand experientially about physical pain; what's normal, what's not, what to do with whichever it is and even how to physically feel again.

Note - As you walk in a peaceful (or at least a lot more peaceful) world with this new life of yours, you may go weeks even months on an even keel with nothing from the jungle surfacing. It's possible that something along the way may trigger a jungle reaction. This is not to say all the work you did was incomplete. It simply means you stumbled over an old land mine that wasn't discovered before.

If old tactics (ROE rules) or distorted thinking patterns flair up again, relax you do HAVE TIME. As you did before, evaluate the "tactic(s)" or thinking, compare it to today and see if it needs to be changed or modified to become more accurate and adult. Even with the chance that a surplus unexploded land mine is "out there", no need to panic. It won't kill you and believe it or not, you're still SAFE. You'll deal with it if—and when—you come across it.

Keep purposefully and intentionally connecting with another human being(s). It often does get easer with experience and practice. Even if there is always a bit of awkwardness to it, continue to learn modern ways to keep your heart safe.

Two additional forward-looking goals to address (if you haven't already):

First. Take on the "Who I am . . . really?" question. Not "who you need to be"; not "who others wanted you to be"; not "what you had to be in order to survive": The "who" you were born to be if you hadn't been thrown into a jungle-like war zone. Some possible ways to aid this endeavor along are the various personality, strengths and gifts inventories that are readily available.

With my clients I suggest they make several lists (not all at the same time and in no particular order either). I want them to collect data about themselves:

1. What do I LIKE . . . and DON'T LIKE

Even things like, what color do I really like? What kinds of apparel do I really like or don't like. Do I really like the sport or activity I've been doing for years? Not "what was needed to help me survive". Take the list any direction you want and however you want. And if you're not sure, put it down anyway, you can always add or erase it as you go.

2. What I WANT and things I really DON'T WANT

Many times RAD people learned to stop wanting and have to learn how to dream again—maybe a new skill to learn.

3. What am I (or think you are) good at skill-wise and what am I not good at skill-wise (or so you think).

Here is where time with friends, a support group, a small group and/or therapy may help discover these realities. There's no right or wrong way, whatever will work for you personally. Think of it as "growing up."

Second. Take the time and effort to learn how to relax—physically, mentally and emotionally. Learn to take care of yourself—which are modern ways to keep SAFE. Here again is where a therapeutic massage, relaxation techniques and/or deep breathing skills can be helpful.

The "Big Tired"

If you haven't felt a physical sense of exhaustion yet, it's likely you will during this phase of the healing journey. The emotional work it took to get out of the RAD jungle can exhaust the physical body. Add this to the body's realization that the war might really be over now and the body itself may begin to let down from going full speed in survival mode and want to collapse in a pile of exhaustion. I don't have numbers for this phenomena, still I have witnessed it enough times to realize it's a part of many clients' journey. If you are experiencing an increased level of tiredness, don't be surprised; it's a part of the journey. It will take time and it's do-able even as an adult.

IV.   CONCLUDING THOUGHTS

I am restating two things. The purpose for this book is to help you understand more accurately what the inside world is like for RAD whether officially—or unofficially—diagnosed. The other is this journal represents circumstances from real people, all of which have been teens or older. Still, a good amount of the thinking process and patterns are present to some degree in a child with RAD. I have attempted to collect and simplify the most usable data on the subject.

Lastly, one more restatement, I'm not here to lay out a specific treatment plan that will fit every person, rather a listing of several therapeutic issues to be sure and address somewhere along the way.

If you're the RAD person; you made it this far, now let's get you "home" . . . safely home.

BIBLIOGRAPHY

Wilder, James. Banana Baseball, DVD, Directed by The Life Model, http://www.lifemodel.org/index.php, 2005

Sanford, Timothy. "I Have to be Perfect" And Other Parsonage Heresies. Colorado Springs, CO: Llama Press, 1998

Stoop, David. Hope for the Perfectionist. Nashville, TN: Thomas Nelson, Inc., 1991

Sanford, Timothy. Losing Control and Liking It. Colorado Springs, CO: Focus on the Family / Tyndall. 2009.

Stewart, Donald, Refuge. Birmingham, AL: New Hope Publishers, 2004.

Victoroff, Jeff, M.D., Saving the Brain, Bantam Books, New York NY, 2002

Wilson, Sandra, Ph.D., Hurt People Hurt People. Grand Rapids, MI: Discovery House Publishers, 2001.

Cline, Foster and Fay, Jim. Parenting with Love and Logic. Colorado Springs, CO: Pinon Press, 1990.

Gray, Deborah. Attaching in Adoption. Indianapolis, IN: Perspectives Press, Inc., 2002

Purvis, Karyn Ph.D. and others. The Connected Child. New York: McGraw-Hill, 2007

Cloud, Henry and Townsend, John. Safe People. Grand Rapids, MI: Zondervan, 1995

Seamands, David. Healing for Damaged Emotions. Colorado Springs, CO: David C Cook Publishing, 1981

END NOTES

1 American Psychiatric Association: Diagnostic and Static Manual of Mental Disorders, Fifth Edition (Arlington, VA: American Psychiatric Association)

2 "Erikson's stages of psychological development," Wikipedia, http://www.en.wikipedia.org/wiki/Erikson's_stages_psycyhological_development (accessed March 14, 2011).

3 Cherry, Kendra. "Hierarchy of Needs: The Five Levels of Maslow's Hierarchy of Needs," About.com Psychology, http://psychology.about.com/od/theoriesofpersonality/a/hierarchyneeds.htm (accessed march 14, 2011).

4 "Erikson's stages of psychological development," Wikipedia, http://www.en.wikipedia.org/wiki/Erikson's_stages_psycyhological_development (accessed March 14, 2011).

5 Bowlby & Ainsworth's Objection Relations / Attachment notes

6 Kelly, Vicky, Ph.D., Sebren Fisher, M.A. (October, 2008). "The Fear-Driven Brain: A Regulation Model for Attachment Disorders", Attachment Disorder Annual Conference, Providence, RI.

7 Joseph LeDoux, The Emotional Brain (New York, NY: Touchstone, 1996)

8 Kelly, Vicky, Ph.D., Sebren Fisher, M.A. (October, 10-13, 2007). "The Fear-Driven Brain: A Regulation Model for Attachment Disorders", 19th Annual ATTACH Conference, Providence, RI.

9 "For the Want of a Nail (Proverb)," Wikipedia, http://www.en.wikipedia.org/wiki/For_Want_of_a_Nail (proverb) (accessed March 24, 2011).

10 VandePol, Bob (June 6-7, 2002) "Critical Incident Stress Management: Basic Training", Colorado Springs, CO.

11 Victoroff, Jeff, M.D., Saving Your Brain (New York, NY: Bantam Dell, 2002).

12 Sanford, Timothy, M.A. (June 20-21, 2003) "Attachment and Trust", World Reunion, Minneapolis, MN.

13 Timothy L. Sanford, M.A., "I Have to be Perfect" and Other Parsonage Heresies (Colorado Springs, CO" LLAMA PRESS, 1998) 112-113.

14 Sanford, 106-108.

15 Victoroff, Jeff, M.D., Saving Your Brain (New York, NY: Bantam Dell, 2002).

16 Scripture taken from the HOLY BIBLE, NEW INTERNATIONAL VERSION. Copyright © 1973, 1978,1984 International Bible Society. Used by permission of Zondervan Bible Publishers.

17 Brazell, Darrell, "Attachment", DVD. Directed by Fireside Productions, Lawrence, KS
http://www.lifemodel.org/index.php:TheLiveModel, 2005

18 Burns, David D., M.D., The Addictive Personality, (Center City, MN: Hazelden, 1996) 10.

19 Webster's New World Dictionary, 2nd College Edition. New York, NY, Simon & Schuler, 1980.

20 Pervus, Karyn B., Ph.D., (December 6-10, 2010). "Created to Connect" Training, Colorado Springs, CO.

CPSIA information can be obtained
at www.ICGtesting.com
Printed in the USA
BVHW041735190219
540658BV00010B/379/P